CUSTOMS

IN

GOD'S HOUSE

REVISED EDITION

BY
ROZ TANDY

Foreword by Dr. Melva Wilson Costen

ISBN: 978-0-615-19926-9

Library of Congress Control Number   2007909175

Unless otherwise identified, Scripture quotations are from the King James
and New International Version of the Bible.

Printed in the United States of America

Roz Tandy
P.O. Box 311023
Atlanta, Georgia 31131
 www.thelukeagency.net
roztandy@thelukeagency.net
(404) 344-1000

DEDICATION

This book is dedicated to the memory of my mother,
Mary Louise Lawrence Marshall, to my maternal
grandparents, Nathaniel and Rebecca Jane Lawrence and
to my uncles, Allen and Julian Lawrence.
It is also dedicated to the memory of my mother in-law,
Hannella Tandy and to my friends, Daphene Evans,
Lori Hodges and George Ray.

They lived the lessons they taught.
They knew that there was good in
Whatever God showed them.
Each understood what the Lord required of them.
These were people of justice
Who loved mercy and who never failed to
Walk humbly with their God.

ACKNOWLEDGEMENTS

My heartfelt thanks to

Tía Ruth

For your constant encouragement and
for always seeing the best in me

Melva Costen

For mentoring and encouraging me and for always challenging
me to go higher, deeper and wider

Ruth Driver, Marsetta Ray and Phyllis Beatles-Jones

For your unending hours of editing,
and writing contributions to this project

Cynthia Durant

For consistently facilitating the *Customer Service in God's House*
workshops with a spirit of excellence

Ronda Flynn Graphics & John Morris-Reihl

For book formatting and cover design

Family and Friends

For your continued prayers, encouragement and support and for
providing me with your many church experiences that are now parts
of this book

CONTENTS

FOREWORD

This exciting revised edition of Customer Service in God's House continues in my estimation as an "epistle to God's flock" on a pilgrimage into the 21st century and beyond! The author, Roz Tandy, is grounded throughout in First Peter as the foundation for her concern. Like other letters of the New Testament identified as "General Epistles," First Peter is addressed to the Church at large, the "flock of God" (5:2), rather than to individual congregations in contradistinction to the letters of the Apostle Paul. Jesus' reference to his disciples as "the little flock" (Luke 12:32) is now the spiritual flock, by virtue of their baptism. This body of Christ has a specific function reflecting the importance of "good stewards of Christ rendering services to the glory of God."

The author demonstrates her familiarity with the Christian's call into the status of a "chosen people" with special privileges that are to be valued and used for the purposes of God at a high level of obedience and service. This particular concern is recorded as follows:

Above all, maintain constant love for one another, for love covers a multitude of sins. Be hospitable to one another without complaining. Like good stewards of the manifold grace of God, serve one another with whatever gifts each of you has received. Whoever speaks must do so as one speaking the very words of God; whoever serves must do so with the strength that God supplies, so that God may be glorified in all through Jesus Christ. To him belong the glory and power forever and ever. (I Peter 4:8 – 11)

Roz Tandy learned practical lessons of liturgical stewardship as a child in church with her family and extended family and as one of four children in a home that continued to be part of the spiritual flock in action. Although I was not present to hear her cry at birth as she entered the world, it has been a joy participating in her growing years and noticing her concern that church folks forget that they are part of God's flock – the household of faith – long before the music stops! Thus, this book, along with her other publications, as well as her workshops and leadership skills, reflects the fulfillment of a call to ministry which Ms. Tandy is currently fulfilling. Readers will rejoice as she skillfully utilizes over thirty-five years of employment in sales, clerical and customer service environments in combination with a lifetime of involvement as a worshiper, teacher and church musician!

In addition to the important service that Customer Service In God's House will provide for lay persons in general, this book is highly recommended as a companion resource for books on the theory, history and practice of Christian Worship and liturgical studies for seminarians and clergy persons, ushers, and church musicians. This recommendation comes from out of my own experiences as a Theological Seminary Professor, Church Musician and as an ordinary member of the flock of God in Jesus the Christ.

Melva Wilson Costen,
Helmar Emil Nielsen Professor of Worship and Music, Emeritus
Interdenominational Theological Center Atlanta, Georgia

INTRODUCTION

Imagine for a moment the following discourse from a recent visitor to your church:

"Thank you for the invitation to worship at your church today. I have heard so much about your beautiful church building and your awesome pastor. I've also heard a lot about the dynamic ministries you have here. You know, my family and I have been out of the church for a while now, and we're looking for a new church home. I know God will eventually direct us to where He'd like us to be. But in the mean time we would still like to worship and become involved with other believers on a regular basis.

*So tell me something. Why should we come to **your** church? There are six other churches within a five to ten mile radius and they all teach the same things that your church does. Their pastors are dynamic and they have some pretty awesome ministries too. So why should my family attend this particular church, and even more importantly what would make us stay?*

Is it ok if I ask your members a few questions?

Congregation, what type of atmosphere will we experience when we enter into the sanctuary? Will we be met with stares and strained smiles from saints who act like they are barely alive? Will the atmosphere seem more like a party with extremely loud greetings and laughter?

Or will we see worshipers lovingly and cheerfully greeting one another while still maintaining an atmosphere filled with reverence and holiness.

And choir members, do you enter the sanctuary with joy and thanksgiving, proud and honored to lead the praise and worship? Or will you saunter into the choir stand as though you are headed to a much-despised job on a Monday morning? Will you exhibit a prideful spirit because you are so talented and have become so popular?

Ushers, do you carry out your duties as doorkeepers of the Lord? Does your countenance reflect that spirit? Will you be attentive and use your discernment as people enter rather than spending that time chatting with your friends, family and fellow ushers/greeters? Will you use wisdom and patience to address me if I ever sit in the wrong section or leave to go to the restroom at an inappropriate time?

I've been struggling for a while now so I don't have many pretty clothes or the appropriate church clothes like a lot of you and I never finished high school. Will your members look down on me?

I'm also married to someone of another race and we've got two small rambunctious children. Will this church receive us without making us feel uncomfortable?

And will I be welcomed with open arms in the different ministries at your church? What is in place here that will help my family discover more of our gifts and talents? Will I be allowed to use those gifts that I am already aware of, or will the leaders be insecure, poorly trained and intimidated individuals who will keep my gifts and me on lock-down?

When I join a ministry will I be adequately trained? I would like to be able to effectively teach other newcomers who may want to be a part of this same ministry.

And you know what? There are lots of skeletons in my closet. I've got a pretty sordid past with some serious issues I've been dealing with most of my life. I need a safe place to open up. How do I know you're not like my last church? They were filled with gossipers that enjoyed spreading everything about everybody.

I've been through so much so I'm learning how to praise my way through a few things. I'm not a quiet worshipper. I am sometimes moved to shout, clap, cry or sing. Will that seem strange to the people at this church? Will they stare at me with a look that says, 'It doesn't take all of that?' My husband on the other hand is an extremely quiet worshipper. He hardly makes a sound. What will they think of him?

At this point in our lives we need some direction and we need to be delivered from quite a lot. Is this church capable of accepting us just as we are? Will you be able to address our needs and ensure that we are consistently being given good spiritual nourishment? We want to be empowered to live this thing called life to its fullest. We have to know that we are sowing our seed on good ground. On Sundays, this family needs more than three points, two poems and a request for 'amens' after every sentence? It's important that we're left with the motivation and encouragement to seek a closer walk with God on our own the other six days of the week.

So tell me…will my family and I get what we need at this particular church or should we continue to look further?"

****

Although you may not hear these concerns voiced aloud, they are very real and need to be acknowledged. You see, it doesn't matter how our church buildings look, what kind of ministries, programs or events are in place. It doesn't even matter how wonderful of an orator the pastor is. If people in need walk through our church doors and the **atmosphere** is not conducive to allowing the Holy Spirit to reign, it's all for naught. The guidance of the Holy Spirit helps keep us as the Body of Christ in order. He is the one who helps us to be better prepared and positioned for those God sends into our churches.

My assignment from the Father is to help prepare the Body of Christ to more effectively receive the masses; those persons who are in need of spiritual support, a church home, deliverance, salvation, healing, teaching, and mentoring. As Christians we must remember that the masses will not necessarily look, act, have been reared or educated like many of us. The masses are also not always made up of those who have been poorly reared or educated or look and act negatively. The masses are those persons outside and also **within** the church who may have heard about Jesus but don't know Him personally and may be curious to find out what the excitement is all about.

After the 9-11 attacks, thousands of people ran to the church. People came in droves – those who had never been and those who had not been in years all came. That should have been one of the church's finest hours. But what happened? Many of our churches were so thrilled to have finally filled up more than 10 pews that they missed the opportunity to bring these people into the kingdom. Some of us were so busy thinking more people meant more money and more people to put on some committee. Some churches even used that moment to make those new comers feel bad about not having shown up sooner or on a more regular basis. Now what happened to all of those people? Why did they stop showing up in church? Why did they go back to their business as usual?

It was the church's responsibility to show them what they had been missing and we failed miserably. But we **will** be given other opportunities because we have not seen the last of the devastating problems this country and the world will face such as September 11th. We've got to be ready. We must learn how to more effectively lift up the name of Jesus so that He can draw the masses in. After they are within our reach we must be equipped to keep them in so that they can be spiritually motivated to become a disciple of Christ. Then they can move on to become a blessing to others.

In order for anything to grow it must first be born. So if the *worldly* are to grow in Christ they must be born again. But before they can even desire a new birth they absolutely must see the benefits or some positive results from those of us already in Christ. We are His advertisement, His billboard. How the world views our treatment to them and to one another has a direct bearing on how anxious they will be to seek a relationship with Christ and to enter into God's House. For those who do come, we must be ready to receive them as they are. Given good instruction over time, their growth will spring forth just like mine did and yours.

So let's continue to run this race with patience for our brothers and sisters already in Christ and for those who are on their way. Let us set the right atmosphere **before** they walk through the doors of our churches and let us never forget why we are all there in the first place.

WHO IS MY CUSTOMER?

If a business has done an incredible job of advertising, you expect to receive just what they said would be delivered. The church has the same obligation when we advertise to the world that *"The Love of Christ is shown here"*. We've got to consistently deliver the goods!

Churches and businesses have two kinds of customers:
- The **internal customers in a business** are the people who work together within that business to keep it running smoothly and profitable. Their job is to ensure the increase and return of new and existing customers.
- The **internal customers in the church** are pew mates, members of the various ministries, church leaders, ministers etc. They are committed to keeping things running smoothly but their most important function is to increase the number of new customers and to make certain that all hindrances are kept to a minimum that would prevent possible new or existing members from returning.
- The **external customers in a business** are the people who purchase goods and services within that business.
- The **external customers in the church** are the visitors, prospective new members, the unsaved, backslidden and those in need of deliverance. Many long-time members of a church also fit into this category. Even the most seasoned saint is a disciple in training. There are always new things to learn to become a more effective witness.

Customer service means exhibiting specific characteristics. It means being:

- Knowledgeable about your organization and its services
- Understanding of the needs of your customers
- Respectful in the way you communicate
- Helpful to ensure the customer gets what he or she needs
- Dependable and able to deliver what is expected
- Honest in your dealings with customers
- Committed to customer satisfaction

Offering good customer service returns certain benefits:

- On-going customer loyalty
- New and repeat customers that will spread the good word
- Customers that will easily forgive when mistakes are made

People offer poor customer service for a number of reasons:

- They don't think it "takes all of that"
- No one has ever told them that what they are offering is not working for them or others
- They rationalize their unacceptable attitudes and behaviors
- They don't know any better

When a customer does not receive the type of service they expect or feel they deserve they will react in one or more ways:

- Complain
- Suffer in silence
- Leave and never return
- Spread the negative word
- Continue to come but always with a bad attitude, looking for something to complain about

NOTES

_____

_____

_____

_____

_____

_____

_____

_____

_____

_____

_____

_____

_____

_____

SINS OF CUSTOMER SERVICE

The saying is true. "You can't please all of the people all of the time", but as Christians we cannot afford to display behaviors that we know could turn someone away. Many times in our churches during worship, meetings, rehearsals etc, we display many of the same attitudes we absolutely dislike seeing in the business *world*.

- **Apathy** – Lack of interest or sensitivity to another's needs
- **Brush-off** – Ignoring or attempting to get rid of a person or his need
- **Robot** – Handling each person the same without discerning the specific needs of an individual or situation
- **Rulebook** – Misinterpreting, misquoting or exploiting policies, scriptures and requirements only to get a point across or to put someone "in check"
- **Runaround** – Passing a person off to someone else to avoid handling the situation personally
- **Coldness** – Being mean-spirited, impatient, unfriendly, moody, inconsiderate etc.
- **Condescension** – Looking down at another because of appearance, finances, vehicle, job, intellect, or a perceived level of spirituality
- **Judgment** – Basing a conclusion solely on what you have seen or heard

NOTES

_____

_____

_____

_____

_____

_____

_____

_____

_____

_____

_____

_____

_____

_____

_____

A LOOK, A LAUGH
AND A LESSON

So many times we go about our activities without regard to how our actions impact others. This is never more important than when we are in the church. Answer these questions related to your own conduct during worship:

- Are you doing what is necessary to make sure that others have a meaningful worship experience, free from unnecessary distractions and annoyances?
- Are you displaying behaviors and attitudes that will make worshippers want to come back and bring others?

Unpleasant situations arise everywhere, including church. Think about the last time you were involved in a not-so-pleasant situation at church.

- Did your response cause the *offender* or the person *offended* to rethink how they currently handle adverse situations?
- Were you like a thermometer - allowing the atmosphere to cause you to feel high or low? Or were you more like a thermostat – you set the atmosphere so that you and others could have a more meaningful worship experience?
- Were you responsible for a person setting a higher, more mature standard for himself because of how you managed a particular situation?

Instructions
Before Reading

There are about 90 different church-related scenarios on the following pages. They are the results of observing over 200 different worship services. These observations along with my own personal church experiences and the personal experiences of others are the basis for this book. Close attention was paid to worshiper interaction before, during and after worship services and during various church-related activities.

This book has been written to provoke healthy discussions among those of us within the church **and** for those who are on their way.

In all likelihood you may know someone who displays any number of the behaviors and attitudes shown; *maybe even you.*

If an individual comes to mind while reading a scenario, attempt to replace the thought of that person with thoughts of yourself. Ask how your own attitudes and behaviors have impacted that same type of situation.

If you have been the offender or the one offended in a way similar to the ones shown, try not to allow any guilt, bitterness or resentment to resurface. Be sure to read and re-read the prayers given for that particular section along with the accompanying scriptures.

Let this book encourage, inspire, convict and bless you so that you can be spiritually, emotionally and physically where God needs you to be.

IT'S NOT WHAT YOU SAY...

It's been said that 90% of conflicts are a result of how something was said to an individual. We must be mindful of a person's personality and possible perception of what we may say before addressing certain situations. Is this person very sensitive or a "cut-to-the-chase kind of person?" Speaking in love means communicating (verbally or non-verbally) so others know you still care even if you disagree.

> *"Be hospitable to one another without grumbling."*
> *I Peter 4:9*

SITUATION: Squeeze play—*"Can you believe all of those people are trying to squeeze in here. Can't they see this pew is already full? I know they may want to sit together but there isn't that much room left with the rest of us who were already here."*

LOOK AT IT THIS WAY: Why not just smile, greet this family and offer to move to another seat with a **genuinely pleasant attitude.** To respond with anything less will not work. Don't pout or use any verbal or non-verbal gestures to draw attention to what you have just experienced. Remember also that when people are attempting to sit on a row where you are seated on the end, you are automatically the "designated pew greeter." No time for judgmental attitudes, negative body language etc. If they are late or on time show them that you are glad they are worshiping with you in the House of the Lord.

SITUATION: That was my spot—*"I know I'm not crazy. I'm sure I placed my purse, Bible and a notebook on this seat to reserve it while I ran to the ladies room. Now someone has come along, moved all of my things and has taken my seat."*

LOOK AT IT THIS WAY: You might as well just greet your new pew mate warmly and sit in your new seat. There is absolutely no point in asking if or why this person moved your belongings and took your seat. You know they did and so do they. What good would it do to confront the guilty party? If they "innocently" ask, "Did I take your seat?" Just smile and tell them that it is perfectly all right and that you will sit right where you are.

SITUATION: Huge hats—*"Lord have mercy. Her son must have given her another one of those three-foot wide hats for Mother's Day. Here she comes, sashaying down front and sitting smack dab in the middle, blocking my view and the view of about 27 other people."*
LOOK AT IT THIS WAY: If she is in the pew right in front of you, just get her attention by saying something nice about her hat, and tell her you're coming to sit next to her (if there is room). Of course, you're really coming up there so you can see. Pray she doesn't put your eye out with her headgear. You can also move to another seat (without pouting). Ladies, if you enjoy wearing large hats, be mindful of others sitting behind and around you and consider sitting in the rear or closest to a wall on an end seat.

SITUATION: The great communicators—*"Those two have to make comments to each other about everything that is either said or sung. Each time they do they lean over which means I can't see the minister or the choir. I feel like I'm at a tennis match."*
LOOK AT IT THIS WAY : If they are seated directly in front of you, why not tap one of them lightly on the shoulder and sweetly say, "Can I get you to lean a little bit more to the left/right so I can see a little bit better. Thank you. I really appreciate it." If that doesn't work just bite the bullet and remember why you are there; to **hear** the Word. But remember, in order to get the most out of it, you can't sulk. You've got to do this with a good attitude.

SITUATION: The sing-a-long —*"Oh, I love this new song the choir is singing. It's my favorite, but I think this man behind me must be a misplaced choir member because he thinks he knows this song and is singing his heart out. Not only is he off key but he is so loud I can barely hear the choir."*

LOOK AT IT THIS WAY: You may want to sit up 'taller' and move forward in your seat just enough to gain this person's attention so he'll take the hint. If it really starts to get to you, turn around and smile. You may want to quietly comment to him that he must really love this song because he is singing his little heart out. Hopefully he'll take the hint. If not, this is again one of many times you'll have to just listen for the message among the madness.

SITUATION: Waiting to exhale—*"Miss Mamie is the sweetest woman in the whole church. As much as I love her, I hate it when she greets me each Sunday because she likes to get right up in my face. Her breath is enough to knock out a mule."*

LOOK AT IT THIS WAY: Take a deep inconspicuous breath, give her a hug and offer her a mint or two…or three or four as you take one for yourself. Just smile, and say to her, "Sweets for the Sweet." Remember don't frown or make faces, and don't share what you have experienced with others.

In a Word…

It's not what you say; it's how you say it.

Look at this statement:
"Woman without her man can do very little."
Do You Agree?
Look at it again:
"Woman, without her, man can do very little"
Now, do you agree?
None of the words changed, but pausing at certain places (because of the added comas) changed the entire meaning of the statement.

PRAYER

Father, You know me better than anyone. Help me to have a more loving spirit toward my brothers and sisters when they do things that differ from what I might do. I need your help so that I won't continue to be so easily irritated or offended by such mundane things. Nothing should distract me and keep me from hearing Your Word and learning more about You.

NOTES

THE SINGLE LIFE

Living single poses its own unique set of challenges. It should come as no surprise that everyone who comes to church is not there just for the Word.

"For thy Maker is thine husband..."
Isaiah 54:5

"As obedient children, not fashioning yourselves according to the former lusts in your ignorance, but as he which hath called you is holy so be ye holy in all manner of conversation;
Because it is written,
Be ye holy; for I am holy."
I Peter 1:14-16

"A man who has friends must himself be friendly but there is a friend who sticks closer than a brother."
Proverbs 18:24

SITUATION: <u>Donny-Wando</u> —*"He looks me up and down like I'm a smothered pork chop, makes inappropriate comments he considers to be compliments and stares at every body part I own. In fact, he has done this each time he sees me at church over the past few months."*

LOOK AT IT THIS WAY: Offer him no encouragement by smiling, acting too sweet and spiritual or by using body language that could be misinterpreted. Be firm but not nasty. Quoting scriptures may not work with this Romeo. Let him know that aside from the fact that he is in church, you find his behavior toward you inappropriate and offensive. If he continues, speak to one or two spiritually mature men at your church and have them speak to him. Refrain from wearing clothing that may place too much emphasize on some of your more "outstanding" physical attributes. You never want to be responsible for distracting anyone from God's Word and attracting what you don't want or need.

SITUATION: <u>Jezzy-Bella</u>—*"She looks at me like I might be a sweet potato cheesecake, makes innuendoes that suggests she thinks I may be her intended, checks me out like she wants to take me home to meet the family, and I don't even know this woman. I've had to put up with this for a while now."*

LOOK AT IT THIS WAY: It looks like she may have claimed you as her significant other. Just as in the previous example, don't encourage this woman especially if she is not who God has chosen for you. Use discretion, and let her know her behavior makes you uncomfortable. If she continues, ask one or two spiritually mature women to speak to her, preferably a married woman such as the minister's wife. This woman may look at another single woman as a jealous competitor. If you are repeatedly approached by someone who says something like, "You're my mate because God showed it to me in a dream," just tell this love-smitten person, "I'm so flattered but I've got to tell you that I don't make a move without asking God first. So let me find out what He has to say about it." And fellows, the same thing holds true for you regarding clothing. You also have to be mindful not to wear those things that you know could possibly distract a fellow Christian from the Word of God.

SITUATION: <u>The loneliest time</u> —*"Doesn't Phyllis have a home of her own to go to? She tries to get our whole family engaged in the longest conversations about absolutely nothing after church almost every Sunday. She acts like she doesn't want to go home."*

LOOK AT IT THIS WAY: For many singles, going home after church is one of the loneliest times of the week. This is especially true for those who have no family or close friends near by. Sunday afternoon is traditionally a time for families to get together, have dinner, to watch sports or the like. A singles' ministry could be creative and come up with some times of sharing to include those who have no connection to family or good friends. This is also an opportunity for all of us in the Body to be more aware and open to those who have this kind of need. Invite them over for dinner and don't forget the holidays.

In a Word...

Many singles view church as an opportunity to meet other singles. In itself, that's not a negative thing; church is an excellent place to meet good friends and build wholesome relationships. But, meeting others cannot become the overriding motivation and activity in attending church. Also, the way singles approach potential new friends is just as important. No one should impose his or her own expectations for a relationship on another person too fast or when it is not mutual. We must always be sensitive to the feelings of singles and non-singles and be patient in cultivating friendships that may become lasting ones.

PRAYER

God, I don't want to be alone anymore. I want to be married, have a family or at least be attached to a potential mate. I'm sorry to say that I get impatient waiting on You sometimes. Help me to stop following my feelings, and instead let me listen for Your guidance and direction. Help me to stay focused on the assignment(s) You have given me and to learn to appreciate and enjoy my singleness.
I know that by doing Your will and waiting on You I will be an even more desirable mate.

NOTES

_____

_____

_____

_____

_____

_____

_____

_____

_____

_____

_____

_____

_____

_____

_____

_____

INSECURITIES

Anytime we allow the accuser of the brethren to redirect our focus it can very easily affect others as well as us. Mass confusion can arise and cause our perception to be totally off base.

> *"There is a way that seems right to a man,*
> *but its end is the way of death."*
> Proverbs 14:12

SITUATION: <u>Protection</u>— *"Here they come again smiling and pretending that they're speaking to me but I know they are only trying to get my spouse's attention. These singles around here aren't fooling me. I guess I need to give them 'the eye' and hold on a little tighter to my mate. Maybe they'll take the hint."*

LOOK AT IT THIS WAY: Ladies and gentlemen, if you are guilty of this kind of conduct, just think how this must make a person feel who just wants to worship and not steal your mate. Who wants to be subjected to that treatment each time they come to church? Please make every attempt to refrain from bringing insecurities and distorted perceptions into your place of worship that could insult and offend others.

SITUATION: <u>Have you been talking about me *again?*</u> — *A woman to a group of her church members as she enters a church meeting: "I know you all were talking about me. I heard someone call my name."*

LOOK AT IT THIS WAY: Even if they have been talking about you, unless you heard the conversation, there is no way to be absolutely sure if they were speaking negatively about you. Learn to take the high road. While you're traveling ask yourself if what you "think" they were saying about you is actually true. If you've determined it is, then continue down that same high road and consider what needs to be addressed in your life in order for you to handle these kinds of situations in a more mature manner.

ON THE OTHER HAND: If you are busy taking care of the Father's business, let them talk. That means you're about something and you're right where you need to be. It's sad, but many church-going saints will spend good valuable time in an attempt to find something wrong with those God is pleased with. Remember, they talked about Jesus so being like Him means being talked about in all kinds of ways.

In a Word...

When a person is insecure, he can imagine that any number of negative attitudes is aimed at him. Try to develop a healthy perspective of yourself so that you don't fall prey to wild imaginations. Develop a habit of inclusion by smiling easily and often at everyone you meet. Don't allow yourself to become suspect of the intentions of others. If unchecked it can result in paranoia. Always remember that you were created to love yourself and others, just as you love the Father.

PRAYER

*Lord, I don't know why I'm so fearful and so insecure.
Show me how to trust You more. I must learn to use the authority
you have given me to put satan under my feet when he whispers
those things that make me doubt my mate's love and fidelity.
Please forgive me for mistreating others by letting my insecurities
get the best of me. To continually see myself as the victim is
certainly not where You need me to be. Help me to always take the
high road.*

NOTES

_____

_____

_____

_____

_____

_____

_____

_____

_____

_____

_____

_____

_____

_____

_____

_____

YOUNG PEOPLE

God has placed many gifts and talents in our young people along with an abundance of energy that can be hard to manage at times. These precious ones are our present and our future. They must be handled with care.

"And they brought unto him infants that He would touch them; but when His disciples saw it, they rebuked them. But Jesus called them unto Him and said, suffer little children to come unto Me, and forbid them not; for of such is the kingdom of God."

Luke 18:15-16

"A man has joy by the answer of his mouth, and a word spoken in due season, how good it is!"
Proverbs 15:23

SITUATION: <u>Party over here</u>—*"I know how it is to be a teenager and want to sit in the back of the church with your friends. But those teens are just sitting back there so they can talk and write notes. They are really starting to get on my nerves with all of that chatter and paper rattling."*

LOOK AT IT THIS WAY: Why not turn around with a pleasant but firm expression (give them the old eyebrow lift with a smile) and say to them that they must respect others who came to hear the Word so you would like them to stop the chatter. Encourage them to listen by offering a pizza party or a few bucks if they can answer questions (prepared by you) about the minister's message. Be creative. The last thing you want to do is to discourage teens from attending church or encourage a rebellious spirit by mishandling a situation. Let them know the behavior that is expected but most importantly, let them know you care.

ON THE OTHER HAND: Don't forget how much you **really** paid attention in church when you were a teen. It's always good to remember when.

SITUATION: <u>Tiny little noise makers</u>—*"That woman has the cutest little boys but she lets them cry and make all kinds of noise before she even thinks about taking them out. And isn't one of them a little special? His parents should know this church can't accommodate that child with all of those problems. No wonder half of the church turns around and frowns whenever they come. I really think they should consider finding another kind of church to attend."*
LOOK AT IT THIS WAY: And what kind of church would you suggest? I would suggest one that actually practices the love of Jesus. It's hard for little ones (without special needs) to sit quietly in church. It's even harder for their parents to have to handle the stares and frowns when their little ones become fidgety. Why not be the worshiper who carries the candy on a stick, the crayons and paper just for times like these. And don't forget to pack some extra love and patience. Many of these parents have so much going on that they can't remember to bring a lot of these much-needed items. Turning around to frown is not helping this situation so why not go up to these parents with a big smile, open arms and offer to hold or take a crying child out for a walk. Oh, you think the little tot will start hollering all over the place if you try to take him/her. Remember they're already making all kinds of racket now. So just take 'em on out and let 'em holler (outside). This parent probably needs the Word a lot more than you do at that moment and what would impress God more; sitting there mad because you're being disturbed or going to the aid of someone in need. Here is something else to consider. Many of these parents are already so frustrated, that having their little one disturb that piece of peace they find at church can be almost too much. Do the right thing. A situation like this could escalate into something devastating.

SITUATION: <u>But they're so young</u> — *"I agree that the youth need to be more involved in the church but I don't think we should have them doing really important things. Only the adults should do that."*

LOOK AT IT THIS WAY: How will our children become better equipped if they are not given opportunities to learn? Adults within our churches must understand that there is no such thing as a junior Holy Spirit created just for children. God has put the same Spirit in them as He has placed in adults. When children are respected and given opportunities along with good instructions from adults, they can begin to recognize when they are being lead of Him in order to lead others.

In a Word...

Everyone can remember a time when the wailing of a child pierced the subdued atmosphere of a worship service. It seemed that all heads turned to see the source of the disturbance. It's a natural occurrence; there's no way to avoid it. Children are with us and must begin to experience regular attendance at church. They will sometimes be noisy, fidgety and cranky. It's an excellent time for you to practice patience. Remember, Jesus said, "Suffer the little children to come unto me." Certainly, we should have the same attitude about our precious little ones.

Teenagers are a different challenge. With hormones raging and so many things going on in their lives, it may be difficult to stay focused on just what is going on inside the church. We've all been there; let's try to remember what it was like for us. Try to bring them to attention in a way that won't thoroughly turn them off. Remember that everyone including our youth should be respected. Allow God to direct you fully when relating to these young people.

PRAYER

Father, as hard as I try I still keep failing. I need more of the fruit of the spirit, especially long suffering. Help me to be more sensitive to the youth and to heed Your voice when You tell me to speak to or assist in ways that may make me uncomfortable. Remind me of my own shortcomings, and let me remember how I sometimes acted as a young person. Thank You, God for being so loving and patient with me. Help me to strive to do the same for others.

NOTES

_____

_____

_____

_____

_____

_____

_____

_____

_____

_____

_____

_____

_____

_____

_____

_____

Our Seasoned Saints

Elderly people are sometimes faced with situations that we all may have to confront one day. Physical and mental frailties are just a few of those things our seniors experience. The loneliness sometimes has been more of a friend than some of us. These are the people who helped pave the way for so many of us in so many ways. We've got to treat them with a lot more love, respect and patience.

"'Rise in the presence of the aged, show respect for the elderly and revere your God. I am the Lord." Leviticus 9:32

"Gray hair is a crown of splendor; it is attained by a righteous life." Proverbs 16:31

SITUATION: <u>Hurry it up, Granny!</u> — *"I just don't believe she needs to walk that slowly. I know she's old but this is ridiculous. She needs to hurry it up. I'm trying to get to my seat too. Oh no! It looks like she's going to sit next to me again this Sunday. I'm not holding that hymn book and Bible up to her face again. She can't be that blind."*

LOOK AT IT THIS WAY: If you have been blessed to see the age where your sight has grown dim and your limbs aren't as nimble as they used to be you are indeed blessed. Pray that if you live to see your seventies, eighties or nineties, that there will be patient, loving people around you at all times. None of us knows what condition we may have to endure. Sow good seeds while there is time.

In a Word...

How often do we actually see our elderly members other than at church? Are we concerned about what happens to them the other six days of the week? How can you be sure that they are being lovingly cared for?

When an elderly member is hospitalized it's easy to make those visits that first or second week (along with every one else.) But do we still check in on them after they have been out of the hospital for six weeks, six months, etc.

Be sure to put a ministry in place within your church to insure that these seniors are being cared for. Never ignore what could be signs of possible abuse or neglect. (Bruises, soiled and unkempt clothing, body odor, always a sad countenance and always alone, etc)

Here are some suggestions to brighten up the life of an elderly person

1. Bring a meal over every now and then and eat with them
2. Go to the grocery store and buy a week's worth of healthy lunches and snacks
3. Walk their dog or bring your *friendly* pet over to visit
4. Clean the gutters
5. Mow their lawn
6. Clean their bathroom
7. Take pictures of them and with them
8. Help send out Christmas cards and include the picture you took of them
9. Get youth to help decorate for Christmas and take down decorations
10. Visit and make a note of what may be needed
11. Help them de-clutter their home room by room
12. Make them a memory book, using photos and stories shared

PRAYER

Father God, I thank you for these beautiful seasoned vessels that I am blessed to have all around me. Help me to revere and honor them as Your word says. Forgive me when I have been impatient and insensitive to these precious ones. I pray that I will gain a fraction of wisdom and knowledge that lies within them.

NOTES

_____

_____

_____

_____

_____

_____

_____

_____

_____

_____

_____

_____

_____

_____

_____

_____

STAYING FOCUSED ON THE REAL ISSUES

There isn't much that can stop us when we've got the right attitude and there's not much that can help us when we don't. It's entirely up to us which direction we allow our attitudes to take us.

"A soft answer turns away wrath; but a harsh word stirs up anger."
Proverbs 15:1

"Judge not, that you be not judged. For with what judgment you judge, you will be judged; and with the measure you use, it will be measured back to you."
Matthew 7:1-2

SITUATION: <u>Now is not a good time</u>—*"It was praise and worship, one of my favorite parts of the service. There I was, lifting up holy hands to the Father, praising His name and singing my heart out, with tears streaming down my face. Anyone should have been able to see that I was in the spirit. I was right there in the Throne Room in the presence of God and then all of a sudden here comes this tap, tap, tap, 'Excuse me, please. Do you mind if I sit here?' I couldn't believe it."*

LOOK AT IT THIS WAY: The best and quickest way to get back into God's presence is to greet this person with a genuine smile and a hug and let them enter into your pew as you re-enter into His presence.

ON THE OTHER HAND: We should all be mindful of where others are "spiritually" when we approach them to be seated. Be willing to look for another seat or wait for a more opportune time to slide into the pew.

SITUATION: <u>Dressed, but not for success</u> – *"They must have come straight from the night club. Look at how short her dress is. If it were any shorter it would be a belt. And that one right there has on pants so tight she'll have to have them surgically removed. What makes people think they can come to church dressed like that?"*
LOOK AT IT THIS WAY: At least they are in the house of God which is the place where they should be accepted and loved just as they are. It should also be the place where these women will learn how to dress more appropriately over time. You must first catch a fish before you can properly *dress* it. Let these ladies first see how much you care about where they are spiritually. Over time they will learn by example the benefits of dressing in a different manner.

SITUATION: <u>The some-timer's</u>— *"Here they come making their grand holiday entrance. They only show up at church on Christmas, Mother's Day and Easter. Would you look at them strolling down the middle aisle waving and grinning like they're in a parade or something? It just makes me sick to my stomach to watch. I think I'll just stay home and let them have my seat on the holidays. I'd rather do that than to look at these phony Christians."*
LOOK AT IT THIS WAY: What do you think Jesus' response would be? I think He would be delighted that they came at all. His greatest disappointment would be with those Christians who look down on these infrequent worshippers. Those of us who are regular churchgoers should attempt to make these people feel comfortable so that they might want to come back on a regular basis. This is the perfect opportunity to show them what they have been missing. Upturned lips, eye rolls, frowns and judgmental attitudes certainly would not make anyone want to keep coming back.

SITUATION: <u>This is not my kind of music</u> – *"Another hymn? Why can't our choir learn some other kind of music? Every church is singing contemporary songs except ours. We need to get with it."*
LOOK AT IT THIS WAY: The scriptures say to praise God with song and to *"...sing praises with understanding." Psalms 47:7* That does not necessarily mean that God would rather hear hymns over contemporary music or the reverse. The purpose is to bring praise and adoration to God which in turn helps us to better understand and embrace His loving character. If your preference is for a particular

type of music, why not purchase a few of those kinds of CD's. That way you can praise God using the music you personally like best. By doing so, you will be able to bring a much more joyful attitude into the corporate worship service. When your praise and worship is sincere God will open you up to appreciate all kinds of ways to adore Him.

ON THE OTHER HAND: No church can or should attempt to please everyone's individual taste in music but some effort could be made to introduce and expose the congregation to the different musical gifts they may not be accustomed to. Worshipers can then develop a better appreciation for other styles of praise and worship music.

In a Word...

It is definitely the case that some people attend church only once or twice a year and on those special occasions, sometimes arrive late or interrupt us with their arrival. It's another test of our own maturity. Isn't it a blessing that these souls are coming out to join us in the worship experience. If we become annoyed quickly by people or when things are not to our liking we are the ones that need to learn the lesson. Try to view them as God surely does, with an abundance of love and acceptance.

PRAYER

God, I did it again. I don't mean to be so judgmental and so super spiritual but I just can't seem to help it. I want so much to love others like I want to be loved, but it's so hard, Lord.
Forgive me for thinking that my way is always the best way.
Provide me with the grace to be an effective witness and an example for others to follow. I know I can't do this by myself.

NOTES

_____

_____

_____

_____

_____

_____

_____

_____

_____

_____

_____

_____

_____

_____

_____

SUBDUE THE FLESH

Do you remember Flip Wilson's comeback whenever he, as 'Geraldine,' was caught doing something wrong? *"The devil made me do it"*, was his usual response. Well-meaning Christians sometimes do the very same thing. But instead, we blame much of our questionable behavior on the Holy Spirit.

"For to be carnally minded is death. But to be spiritually minded is life and peace.... So then, those who are in the flesh cannot please God."
Romans 8:6; 8

"Let all things be done decently and in order."
I Corinthians 14:40

SITUATION: Test-of-my-patience-mony— *"First giving honor to God, who is the Head of my life, greetings to the pastor, saints and friends. It's so good to be in the house of the Lord one more time. I could have been on a cooling board or on a bed of pain... Now, I know the pastor said to give only a 2-minute testimony. But let me tell you right now, that's going to be hard. I just have to tell you what the Lord has done for me over these last twenty-some-odd-years. Let's see now. I think it all started back in January 1985 or was it 1986.* **Hortense!! Which was it?** *(Worshiper yells out to his wife who is sitting in the congregation) Anyway, it was about 5 below zero that day. It hadn't been that cold since I was a young lad in Chicago in 1965... Well saints, I got up out of the bed that morning, took my bath, and put on my favorite shirt and pants. You know the striped green shirt with the brown corduroy pants. I got dressed and went downstairs into the kitchen and fixed some bacon and eggs and then I made myself some hot tea. Wait a minute. I'm sorry. That's not what I had. I made pancakes and I had coffee..."*

LOOK AT IT THIS WAY: Because God is so good it is sometimes easy to get carried away and want to tell everything when giving a testimony. But suppose every saint decided to go over the time limit and mention every tiny detail. First of all it means having an unsubmitted spirit that can cause confusion in the Body. Others may think they can also give too long of a testimony, while some will end up tuning out what could have and should have been a blessing to them. Just tell the "glory part." That's the part that brings glory to God and blesses and encourages the listeners. God is a God of order. He has put people in place to help carry out those guidelines that will help to keep His order in place.

SITUATION: <u>Praise through intimidation</u> — The following is what a praise leader is **shouting** to the congregation while standing in the pulpit with hands on hips, a frown and a not so pleasant tone of voice. *"Ok people. It's praise and worship time. If God's been good to you, you'd better get up out of your seat right now, stand on your feet, and give Him some praise. Don't keep sitting there!!! GET UP NOW!!!"*

LOOK AT IT THIS WAY: And you are still sitting there too scared to get up and too scared to remain seated. As praise and worship leaders we have to make certain that we are totally immersed in the Spirit and that no flesh is showing. How do you know that person who is sitting didn't have an awesome praise session before they even got to church? They may be sitting and just meditating and listening to God for further instructions. They may even have some physical condition that prevents them from standing. Corporate prayer and praise is powerful and greatly needed. But to intimidate others in an attempt to force them to "where you are" is a quick way to have people deliberately arrive at church after praise and worship is over or to skip church altogether. That would certainly defeat the purpose.

ON THE OTHER HAND: If a person who didn't know Christ watched others around him praising God with no outward signs of joy (i.e. smiling, clapping, weeping etc) do you think they would want any of that?

SITUATION: <u>The amplified amen and hallelujah corner</u>—*"Our minister is so awesome and his sermons certainly deserve 'amens' and 'hallelujah's' but some of the people get so carried away that they don't realize how loud and how often they are actually saying it. Sometimes I can't even hear what the minister is saying or what the choir is singing."*

LOOK AT IT THIS WAY: Of course this will happen when worshipers are deeply moved by the Holy Spirit. However, when worshipers *loudly* and *repeatedly* lead the amen corner, causing you and others *not* to hear key points from the message or other parts of the service, you may want to lovingly let them know how this is affecting your worship. Let them know that you can tell they really seem to be getting a lot out of the service, but sometimes their comments get so loud you can't hear what is being said by the minister or other worship leaders. Tell them that they must be totally unaware of it because you know they would never do anything to keep others from hearing the Word. If you find yourself loudly and repeatedly leading the amen corner always do a **Holy Spirit check-up.** Ask yourself if what you are doing is really of Him or if it is simply out of habit or tradition. The Holy Spirit will never allow us to be out of order and keep another from receiving what God is giving.

SITUATION: <u>Can I get an amen?</u> — *"I came to tell you of the goodness of the Lord. Can I get an amen? Our God is a good God. Can I get an amen? Church, hasn't He been good to you? Can I get an amen, Praise Him church! Can I get an amen? Can I get an amen? Can I get an amen? Can I get an amen? ..."*

LOOK AT IT THIS WAY: It is a wonderful feeling to know that people are listening to what God has poured into you by their response. But an anointing is not necessarily given just to get an immediate and audible response from people. More importantly it is given so that the people of God will be empowered after hearing, receiving and applying the Word which will then allow them to go and impact the lives of others. When the message is from God and you are allowing the Holy Spirit to direct how you impart that message to His people, it will be heard. Remember to love the people and not just the crowd.

SITUATION: **A director's right hook**—*"Margaret, what on earth happened to your eye? It's black and blue and swollen shut." "Well, our choir director got a bit carried away directing us last Sunday at church. His arms were flailing all over the place. I was paying close attention to him but before I could duck he mistakenly hit me right in the eye."*

LOOK AT IT THIS WAY: The Holy Spirit is too much of a gentleman to cause us to bring about physical hurt or pain to others. As in the previous examples it is imperative that we keep our flesh in check. What we want others to experience during worship is an outpouring of reasons and opportunities to honor, praise and thank our God.

SITUATION: **Dancing with my Father?** — *It's praise and worship time and they're singing your favorite upbeat praise song. You're moving with the music and getting a little carried away. Before you realize it you've broken out into a sweat, closed your eyes and moved into the aisle and you are doing the "Bump" with one of the ushers.*

LOOK AT IT THIS WAY: It looks like you are moving with the beat of the music and not the Spirit. Praise and worship music can sometimes make you want to "holler and throw up both your hands." But we've got to be careful because that groove to the beat of the music can sneak up on you. We never want a person to witness the type of dancing in the church that simply looks like a Saturday night in the club. Remember even animals can dance when they hear music. But what separates us from them and the world is that we dance in praise and honor to our Heavenly Father.

SITUATION: **Sneakin'-Preachin'**— *"Good morning church. Pastor Ellington has asked me to share just one or two highlights about our building campaign with you. But I'm sure he won't mind if I take a few **additional** minutes to say how some of you are going straight to Hell in a hand-basket if you don't start giving more. Turn with me to Malachi. Would a man rob God? Now, please turn with me to these six other scriptures God has laid on my heart..."*

LOOK AT IT THIS WAY: Is there an appointed and anointed woman or man of God already in place to deliver the morning message? If so, be absolutely certain that God has opened this particular door for you to share your message with the church. We cannot allow our excitement to reveal what God has laid on our hearts in an untimely manner. If the timing is off your message may not be received as it should be.

SITUATION: <u>Unbalanced</u> — *First person: "We have a good time at my church on Sundays. At each of our Sunday services the choir sings for about an hour, **everyone** in the church gives a 10-minute testimony and we always take at least 30 minutes to do a few "holy dances" before the pastor's sermon." Second person: "Every Sunday at our church we go through about 25 long scriptures in detail and we listen to our pastor's two hour sermon. We never leave church before 5pm."*

LOOK AT IT THIS WAY: There is absolutely nothing like the experience of a 'spirit-filled' worship service, where the Holy Spirit moves you beyond human comprehension. Neither is there anything wrong with being fed the wonderful all-encompassing Word of God. Worshippers should leave a service filled with enough Word to get them through a week that could be saddled with unexpected trials and tribulations and enough spirit to seek His presence in the comfort of their own home, car or office. All spirit and no word could make an unsaved or unchurched individual feel totally left out, not understanding what was happening around them. *("Else when thou shalt bless with the spirit, how shall he that occupieth the room of the unlearned say Amen at thy giving of thanks, seeing he understandeth not what thou sayest?" I Corinthians 14:16-17)* A service with word only and no spirit might cause the most energetic person to struggle to stay alert and others not to receive. God is a God of order and balance. He requires us to be sensitive to unbelievers and others seeking spiritual maturity in our worship gatherings. We must always be guided by the Holy Spirit to ensure our worship will be a blessing to those who came to receive and a pleasant surprise to those who didn't.

In a Word...

It's amazing the things that get credited to God, or more accurately blamed on God. We must be mindful of the fact that many times we are acting according to our own will and therefore can often be in error. The liberty of worship doesn't mean we cast off all restraint. The worship experience should be genuine and free, but it should also be orderly as directed by the Holy Spirit. He will never cause us to act in a way that is rude, inconsiderate or that is a distraction from His word and direction.

PRAYER

God, as much as I try, I still keep 'sliding' over into the flesh realm. I don't want to grieve your Holy Spirit by not being in tune to Your directions. As a Christian, I have been appointed to help equip the saints and those who have not yet reached up to You. Father, this is an awesome task that I am honored to have, so help me to peel back my flesh when it tries to show. Whatever I do must be pleasing in Your sight and must not be done for form or fashion, to tantalize emotions or to bring more attention to myself. I ask for forgiveness for those times that I have been thinned skinned and defensive when others lovingly rebuked me for my behavior. I thank You for their boldness, their love and for this special time of growth in my life.

NOTES

_____

_____

_____

_____

_____

_____

_____

_____

_____

_____

_____

_____

_____

_____

_____

SUBMITTING TO AUTHORITY

Don't you hate those days when nothing seems to go your way? Many times it's because of those things we have or have not put into place. Not submitting to those in authority can cause added stress and confusion to you and others around you.

"Most assuredly I say to you, he who receives whomever I send receives Me; and he who receives Me receives Him who sent Me."
John 13:20

"Let every soul be subject to the governing authorities. For there is no authority except from God. Therefore whoever resists the authority resists the ordinance of God, and those who resist will bring judgment on themselves."
Romans 13:1-2

SITUATION: <u>This service is not going according to *my* plan</u>—
"Bishop Hill isn't even preaching today and I invited my co-workers to hear him. I know they don't want to hear his wife, Marilyn preach. We might as well leave. We'll come back next week when he returns."
LOOK AT IT THIS WAY: Remain in submission if the service does not go the way you were expecting. If your minister of choice is not delivering the message, maintain a respectful attitude toward the person who is. Imagine how it will look to a visitor or to an immature Christian if you were to get up and leave? Here's something else to think about. If the minister is guided by the Holy Spirit, it may result in an abbreviated or lengthened message or no morning message at all. It may mean only praise and worship, a healing or deliverance service, holy dancing, or the like. Take part in the service. Never come for just one or two special parts, and

never disrupt the flow of the Holy Spirit by having a rebellious attitude because things did not go the way you planned. When you come to receive, you always will.

SITUATION: **But I want to leave NOW!** — *Woman to usher," I don't see why I can't leave now. I've already accepted Jesus and I've been a member of this church for years. I'm just trying to avoid that crowd in the parking lot. Why do I have to stay and watch these people walk to the altar? Besides, I had my finger up, head bowed down and I was tiptoeing."*

LOOK AT IT THIS WAY: And you are still out of order! You heard the minister ask that there be no movement or talking at this point in the service. You were also aware of the usher who motioned for you to remain seated. It is extremely important that every Christian know those things that could distract or interrupt a move of the Holy Spirit. Submitting is not a power play. It keeps the order of God in place. Ask yourself if you want to be the one responsible for interrupting the move of the Holy Spirit at a crucial time that could result in someone NOT giving his or her life to Christ.

SITUATION: **I'm staying right here**—*"But I parked here last week and nobody said anything. Besides, you're only a parking attendant. You are not the minister. I'm parking here anyway."*

LOOK AT IT THIS WAY: Many of us think the parking lot attendants don't have a clue when they direct us into certain parking spaces. But you weren't at that meeting where they outlined each parking space and came up with a good workable plan that they expect you to follow. Parking attendants are some of the hardest workers and least respected by the Body of Christ. They come early, miss the service many times to make sure the parking lot is secured and they stay late helping many of us unlock car doors because we've locked our keys inside. When they are assisting you, begin to look at them as God does; a committed, loyal servant and friend of the King.

SITUATION: But I like *this* seat—*"But why can't I sit up front where the ministerial staff sits. There are plenty of extra seats. God is no respecter of persons so it's not right for them to be the only ones to be up front in the good seats."*

LOOK AT IT THIS WAY: In most cases ministers sit near the front so that the senior minister can easily and readily find them in case they are needed. If this situation or a similar one becomes problematic try not to air your concerns in the midst of a church service. This could easily result in drawing attention to you while distracting others from the worship service. Stay in submission while praying for greater understanding.

ON THE OTHER HAND: Wouldn't it be wonderful if our churches would consider reserving the so-called *best* seats for first time visitors, the physically impaired or for those *considering* salvation. And wouldn't it be great to see one or two leaders up front while the rest were dispersed throughout the worshippers to discern spiritual needs, to pray and encourage. Something to consider...

SITUATION: I already gave at the office—*"I'm not at work! This is the church! I think it's ridiculous to have all of this training and these monthly meetings for church stuff. And can you believe we are actually going to be evaluated every quarter by the ministry leader? We're not getting paid for this. We're volunteers. This isn't some big corporation. It's only the church!"*

LOOK AT IT THIS WAY: Do it all as unto the Lord. If meetings, training and evaluations are good enough to meet the demands of a corporate environment then God's house should certainly receive no less. The workers/servants in the church **must** be properly equipped to help carry out the mission and vision of where they have been assigned. Who would want to be a part of an organization that did not think it necessary to have its members or employees adequately trained and informed?

In a Word...

When you united with your chosen local church, you agreed to follow the rules that were established. You consented to respect those that are placed in authority to bring order to that body of believers. Sometimes the decisions will not be your preference but in the interest of harmony, try to respect the decision. Agree to disagree in love. If you feel it is appropriate to discuss the situation, do so at the right time and in a spirit of respect and humility. Ask God to give you the correct words that will communicate your concern and the willingness to abide with the ultimate direction of the person(s) who are in charge.

PRAYER

Lord, I don't always understand why I should submit to certain people or why or how they got to be in a position of authority. But You do. God, I really want to receive and honor these people as sent from You. Help me not to become envious, jealous or rebellious. Help me to remember that no one gets into power or in a position of authority without Your knowledge.   Remind me that those in authority carry Your appointment even if they do things I may not agree with.

NOTES

_____

_____

_____

_____

_____

_____

_____

_____

_____

_____

_____

_____

_____

_____

_____

_____

_____

_____

BE DOERS OF THE WORD

Each time we speak, act a certain way or display certain body language, someone may be watching or listening to us. That person could very well be someone who is trying to decide if being a Christian is really for them. How do you think your overheard conversations and other actions would sway an undecided person?

"Do not merely listen to the Word and so deceive yourselves. Do what it says. Anyone who listens to the Word but does not do what it says is like a man who looks at his face in a mirror and after looking at himself, goes away and immediately forgets what he looks like. But the man who looks intently into the perfect law that gives freedom, and continues to do this, not forgetting what he has heard but doing it—he will be blessed in what he does."
James 1:22- 25 NI

SITUATION: <u>Forgive and forgive and forgive...?</u>—*"Oh, no. I'm not letting her get away with this again. I know what the Bible says; but it also says to use wisdom. And wisdom tells me that I have given her enough chances already. I don't care if she has apologized. I will not forgive her this time."*

LOOK AT IT THIS WAY: Of course that's **your** interpretation of the scripture. But let's see what God really has to say about the matter of forgiveness. *Matthew 18:21-22 NI "Then Peter came to Jesus and asked, "Lord, how many times shall I forgive my brother when he sins against me: Up to seven times?" Jesus answered, "I tell you, not seven times, but seventy-seven times."* Seventy seven is the number of eternity, meaning we shouldn't attempt to keep track of how many times we forgive someone. We must always forgive those who are repentant, no matter how many times they stumble before us. And remember, you too will have this same need to be forgiven again and again and again and again…

SITUATION: <u>But God knows my heart</u> – *"Ms. Coleman, do you have all of the equipment and food for the children's camping trip today?" "Mrs. Driver, I meant to call you last week. I just didn't have the time to do any of those things I promised to do for the kid's trip today. I've got so many changes going on in my office and you know they're renovating my house, then some of my family dropped in from out of town the other day and now my dog is sick. It was a mistake for me to have taken on this camping trip responsibility. But God knows my heart was in the right place."*

LOOK AT IT THIS WAY: Your heart may be in the right place but people are counting on you so they need more than your good intentions. What is needed now in addition to a correctly positioned heart is action, work, activity, movement. Get the picture?
Look at the following scripture. *"It is better not to vow than to make a vow and not fulfill it. Do not let your mouth lead you into sin. And do not protest to the temple messenger, my vow was a mistake."...Ecclesiastes 5:5 NIV*

SITUATION: <u>Haters in the house</u> – One worshipper to another in the church parking lot. *"Ump! I see you got another car. It looks used to me. Oh, excuse me. I mean it looks **pre-owned**. I didn't see anything wrong with your old car myself. Now, that Mercedes you got right there is a gas guzzler and you're in trouble if it ever breaks down. It'll cost you a fortune. Suppose you lose your job. And didn't they have a recall a few months ago on that same model? If you ask me you should have kept that 1962 Dodge. Sure, we could hear the muffler from a mile away but you could have gotten used to that and there wasn't even that much smoke coming from the tail pipe. Shoot, my brother-in-law could have painted that car for you and it would have been just fine."*

LOOK AT IT THIS WAY: Fine for whom? Why do some of the church saints harbor so much jealousy? Why couldn't this person be glad for the member who was blessed with the **new** Mercedes? It seems as though some people are happy with you and for you as long as you seem down and out and have all of the "props" that go along with that status. How sad! What makes us think God is pleased with this kind of behavior and what makes us think it will speed up those blessings we've been asking for? Don't hate! Celebrate and be happy for those who are being blessed. What better way to prepare for your own "happy dance" when the blessings you've been praying for begin to flow?

SITUATION: <u>Divine restoration</u> — *"Sh-h-h-h. Here he comes. Can you believe he has the nerve to walk back into this church after what he did? He has disgraced his family and this entire ministry. There is absolutely no way he should be allowed to be a part of anything at this church anymore."*
LOOK AT IT THIS WAY: *Galatians 6:1-2 "Brothers, if someone is caught in a sin, you who are spiritual* **(Mature Christians, Christ like, Spirit filled, Holy Ghost led)** *should restore him gently. But watch yourself, or you also may be tempted.* **(Tempted to be judgmental, superior or to get involved in the same kind of sin)** *Carry each other's burden and in this way you will fulfill the law of Christ."* SELAH!!!

SITUATION: <u>Beat to a pulp</u> — **"***Mother Witherspoon really came down hard on us. I agree that we could have made a better decision but she didn't have to yell at us like that in front of everyone. I was feeling bad enough."*
LOOK AT IT THIS WAY: Mistakes will happen. That's an absolute guarantee. But never make a situation worse by publicly discussing a mistake when it is at the expense of a person's dignity. As Christians we must realize when adversity occurs this is the time to teach a lesson. It's a teachable moment. Don't make the mistake of using this same opportunity to become quarrelsome, to condemn or display any hint of arrogance. Remember you are attempting to show others the heart of the One you are prompting them to embrace. *"The Lord God has given me the tongue of the learned that I should know how to speak a word in season to him who is weary." Isaiah 50:4* The learned tongue is the tongue that has learned to listen and say the right things at the right time.

SITUATION: <u>Church has already started??</u> — *"Oh-oh! They're about to take up the offering. I didn't think we were **that** late. Oh well. At least we came."*
LOOK AT IT THIS WAY: Do you make it to work on time everyday? Do you make sure that you are never late getting to the airport for a flight? Then why is it so hard to get to the House of

God on time. Being on time is reverencing God. It means honoring him by using your time effectively. It keeps you from being stressed and having to rush to church disturbing others already in the worship service. But one of the greatest benefits of being on time is not missing any of the wonderful things that have been prepared especially for you.

SITUATION: <u>Parking lot '500'</u>—This is a person's comment after almost being struck by a car. *"Wow! That was close. I almost got hit."* These are the comments made by the person who was driving that same car. *"You need to get out of the way. Can't you see all of these cars trying to get out of the parking lot? And no, I am not waving at you. If you weren't so stupid you would see I'm only using one finger."*

LOOK AT IT THIS WAY: Would you believe that all of this is happening in the church parking lot after a Sunday church service? Believe me, you will still have to wait those 30 minutes in the line at the buffet and you'll only miss five minutes of that football game. The church parking lot is where Christians sometimes seem to dump everything they were just taught in the sanctuary. What's the point in rushing out to an already crowded parking lot? This would be a great time to just sit in the sanctuary and meditate on what you just learned or to greet some of those worshippers you've never met. Don't test God's grace and mercy by driving recklessly in or out of the parking lot. Drive like you really are a child of the King. And remember when driving in or out of a busy parking lot; take a space and then give a space.

SITUATION: <u>Play another tune</u>—*"I'm not 100% sure, but I think Eugene might be a bit confused regarding the gender God intended for him. This is a Bible believing church and we can't have **that** kind of person as our organist no matter how talented he is. We need to get him out of that pulpit making the church announcements on Sunday too. Let's just find somebody who acts like a real Christian to take over Eugene's duties."*

LOOK AT IT THIS WAY: We ALL have and will continue to fall short of where God would have us to be. As Christians we sometimes stress over and dwell on what we might consider as the *obvious* sins and iniquities of others. We seem to forget that God hates ALL sin. What type of organist do you think God would prefer over Eugene; a backbiter, a gossiper, a thief, a person who cheats on their spouse and on their taxes, or one who will not submit to authority? Or do you think God would rather have someone read the Sunday announcements who has *a proud look, a lying tongue, hands that shed innocent blood, a heart that devises wicked imaginations, feet that are swift in running to mischief, or one who is a false witness that speaks lies or one that sows discord among brethren? Proverbs 6:17-19.* You (*continue to*) be the judge but remember that God doesn't love us any more than another because **our** sin may be a hidden or secret sin. He still knows. *Why do you criticize and pass judgment on your brother? Or you, why do you look down upon or despise your brother? For we shall **all** stand before the judgment seat of God. Romans 14:10*

SITUATION: <u>An answered prayer unrecognized</u>— *"Ronald sure does look good. He's gained his weight back, his eyes are bright and his skin looks great. He looks like a movie star. I'm starting to think he was never really sick at all. Nobody looks that good and healthy after an illness like he supposedly had. I believe he just used that 'make-believe' illness to get some attention. This church spent an awful lot of time fasting and praying for him, not to mention all that money we gave to help with his so-called medical bills."*
LOOK AT IT THIS WAY: You asked God to heal Ronald and He did. But maybe God was answering the prayers of someone who actually believes He is Jehovah-rapha, the Lord who heals and that by His stripes we are actually healed. Here's another who didn't recognize an answered prayer. *"And when he* **(Peter)** *had considered the thing, he came to the house of Mary the mother of John...where many were gathered praying.* **(They were praying for his release and safety.)** *And as Peter knocked at the door of the gate, a damsel came to hearken, named Rhoda. And when she knew Peter's voice, she opened not the gate for gladness, but ran in, and told how Peter stood before the gate. And they said unto her, thou art mad. But she constantly affirmed that it was even so. Then said they, It is his angel. But Peter continued knocking; and when they opened the door, and saw him, they were astonished."Acts 12:12-16* If they believed God had answered their prayer they would have been excited but not the least bit surprised to see their pal Peter.

SITUATION: I just wanted to say hi— *"I saw Rev. Harvey talking to Carla after church last Sunday. I just wanted to speak to him but when I headed his way he gave me the coldest look and turned his face from me. I wasn't trying to interrupt his conversation."*

LOOK AT IT THIS WAY: If you're involved in a conversation that is personal or intense, and you don't want to be interrupted you should find a more private area. You are sure to be interrupted in a sanctuary or a hallway full of moving worshippers. It can be annoying when you are continuously interrupted, but not to acknowledge a person who is trying to get your attention will never go over well. You can simply say "excuse me" to the person you are speaking to while smiling and waving to another person. If after you've waved and smiled and that person insists on carrying on a conversation with you, introduce them to the person you were already talking to and tell the other person that you will be right with them as soon as you finish the conversation you are already engaged in. As you are saying that be sure you are smiling and nodding as you move closer to the other person to resume your conversation.

ON THE OTHER HAND: Be mindful not to engage leaders or anyone else in **l—o—n—g** conversations especially when you know others are waiting "their turn" to acknowledge this same person. If you need to share something that could be rather lengthy, why not call the church office and make an appointment, take the person out to lunch, write a letter or send an e-mail.

In a Word...

It's so easy to revert back to our old way of thinking and acting, but scripture tells us that, "Those who are borne of God have overcome the world and...walk in the spirit." That means we strive every day to live the spirit of the Word. The spirit of the Word is loving God and your neighbor. The real test comes in how we consider, react, and respect each other. How can we say we love God who we've not seen and not love or even act like we love our brothers and sisters?

PRAYER

*God, I can't seem to hold onto Your Word. Even after being blessed
by an anointed message I still get so easily irritated and I act
as though I don't even know You sometimes. I study Your Word
every day, but I just can't seem to put it into practice. Help me to let
it soak into my spirit so that I can pass these 'pop quizzes' that
continue to come up. I pray I will begin to act in a way that is
pleasing to you.*

NOTES

_____

_____

_____

_____

_____

_____

_____

_____

_____

_____

_____

_____

_____

_____

_____

_____

HOLD YOUR TONGUE

Contrary to what some may believe gossip is not the delivery of vital information used to inform the uninformed. It is a lethal form of communication. It does nothing to heal, comfort or bring greater love to others. Why is it that so many in the Body are drawn to it?

*"A talebearer revealeth secrets; but he that is of a
faithful spirit concealeth the matter."*
Proverbs 11:13

SITUATION: <u>A prayer circle?</u>—*"Earl, we need to be in prayer for Mike. He's really going through it."* Now that was all that needed to be said. *"You know the police were at his house last night. I think his son, Ryan got into some more trouble. I heard it was drugs again."*
LOOK AT IT THIS WAY: That's why it's called a prayer circle. There should be no break anywhere in it. By sharing too much information, you may be breaking a spoken or unspoken confidentiality agreement. Gossip is gossip. If you and Earl are going to pray for Mike, remember you'll be talking to God and He already knows the details. There is no need to share the 'extras' when you know the possible consequences. Everyone is not mature enough to handle all of the details. It is too tempting and could very easily lead to spreading gossip.

SITUATION: <u>They're leaving in droves?</u>—*"I heard that six more families have left the church. I also heard they moved their membership for the same reason Tommy and Shirley did when they left last year. I know you heard about all of that. Well, in case you didn't let me tell you what happened."*
LOOK AT IT THIS WAY: You don't know the whole story because you weren't involved. You only heard second, third or fourth-handed information. If those leaving a church are following

the leading of the Holy Spirit your job is to wish them well and to continue to pray that God will use them mightily. If you think a person's decision to leave is not of God, then your job is to wish them well and to pray that they will clearly hear from God and follow His direction (not yours) and that God will use them mightily. When God releases worshipers from a particular church or when members "assume" God has released them, be supportive. Let the person know you will continue to pray that they will be led by the Holy Spirit to do all God has for them to do. And by all means, stay in prayer for yourself so that you will know when and if it's time for you to move forward. **One more thing...** When members leave a particular church and come back to that same church to visit, welcome them with open arms as you would any other visitor. Don't make the mistake of giving former members the cold shoulder because you are upset with them for having left. Encourage them to come back for special programs or to drop by when possible. Let them know that you're always glad they came.

SITUATION: <u>You don't know like I know</u>— *"If I were you I wouldn't set foot into that church and I know you aren't thinking about joining there. I was a member at that church for seventeen years but I wised up and left. So sit down and let me tell you a few things you need to know."*
LOOK AT IT THIS WAY: When you leave a particular place of worship to join another, never spread negative well-founded or unfounded information about that church's members, its ministries or minister(s). The negative things you may have experienced could have very well been used by God to further your spiritual growth and to move you to your new place of worship. Never share information that will not uplift the Gospel of Jesus and by all means never attempt to rationalize your need or desire to do so.

SITUATION: <u>I thought you were my friends</u>— A woman named Tracie overhears a group of people talking about some of the things she did before she gave her life to Christ. She **only heard** what they were saying but she **did not see** who was doing the talking. She approaches a man she saw coming from the general vicinity of where she heard the gossip, **not knowing** he was one of the main gossipers. *"Cliff, did you hear how those people were talking about* me back there? I've had it. I'm leaving this church. I might as well go back to exotic dancing in the clubs. I thought the people here would be different. They're just a bunch of hypocrites, like all of the rest of the church people."

LOOK AT IT THIS WAY: The best and most Christ-like response would be to confess—admit it and quit it! Cliff should confess by telling her he was one of the people talking about her. He needs to ask for forgiveness and use this opportunity to tell her about his difficulty with exemplifying a daily Christ-like nature. This opportunity could be used to befriend her with brotherly affection, confess to the other gossipers, tell them what happened and encourage them to also confess and ask for forgiveness. Gossip hurts everyone involved. People who trust us get hurt and may never trust anyone again. Those of us in the Church may have robbed them of the one thing they need most, which is a safe place to open up and be made whole.

In a Word...

The temptation to gossip is a real one, but the truth is gossip appeals to our lower nature and nothing positive ever results from it. As a matter of fact, "good gossip" is an oxymoron. Gossip can cause other people to change their opinions of the person who is the object of the hearsay conversation. At its worst, many people have had their reputations destroyed as a result of gossip. As Christians we are called to lift up and edify others, not destroy them. When someone bringing gossip approaches you with some juicy tidbits, invite the person to join you in prayer for the situation instead. This will keep you on track and discourage the talebearer from approaching another person with the same intent. Remember not to ever start or spread rumors about your church, the members, pastor or any other church, its members or pastor. If you are not willing to lay your life down on what was said, keep it to yourself. You never know the entire story if you were not one of the major players. No matter how flat a pancake is, it still has two sides. Remember also that silence can never be misquoted. Let's adhere to the old adage, "If you don't have something good to say, don't say anything at all."

PRAYER

Lord, I need Your help and Your forgiveness. I have hurt so many because of what I chose to say. Help me to never initiate or repeat those things that do not build up my sisters and brothers. Even if it is true, I pray I will be lead by Your Holy Spirit to keep a guard over my mouth and ears. Keep me from listening to gossip and give me boldness to lovingly rebuke those who come to me with it.

NOTES

_____

_____

_____

_____

_____

_____

_____

_____

_____

_____

_____

_____

_____

_____

_____

_____

CHURCH BULLIES

Who would suspect there would be bullies in God's House? Of course they don't think of themselves as such but anytime we choose certain people to pick on that is exactly what we are.

> *"He gives power to the weak and to those who have no might*
> *He increases strength"*
> Isaiah 40:29

> *"O generation of vipers, how can ye, being evil, speak good things?*
> *For out of the abundance of the heart the mouth speaketh. A good*
> *man out of the good treasure of the heart bringeth forth good things:*
> *and an evil man out of the evil treasure bringeth forth evil things.*
> *But I say unto you, That every idle word that men shall speak, they*
> *shall give account thereof in the day of judgment."*
> Matthew 12:34-37

> *"If anyone among you thinks he is religious, and does not bridle his*
> *tongue but deceives his own heart, this one's religion is useless."*
> James 1:26

SITUATION: <u>You *are* the weakest link. Goodbye!</u> —*"Here comes Brother Jeremy again. He really gets on my nerves. I don't know what it is about him but I just don't like him. No one seems to. He is always trying to fit into somebody's group."*
LOOK AT IT THIS WAY: There is a word that describes those groups he is trying to be associated with. They're called cliques and they have absolutely no place in the house of God. Sure, he may be a nerve plucker. We've all got people in our lives we're glad to see come and there are those we're glad to see go, but God requires us

to welcome the Brother Jeremys of the world with open arms. He belongs just as much as anyone does. It is our job to encourage him so that he begins to recognize his own strengths and gifts from God. Anyone can be transformed when shown the consistent love of Christ. *"Seeds of greatness lie buried within unpromising people that abruptly spring to life when they are recognized, watered and nurtured."*

SITUATION: <u>Mean mouthing</u>—*"Sister Odell should know her solo days are over. She just needs to come up out of that choir stand and sit herself down with the rest of us. And some of those praise dancers should know that they are not the right size to be up there twirling and prancing around like that. And Brother Roscoe gets on my last nerve always claiming to have written some of the songs the choir sings. He doesn't have a creative bone in his body."*
LOOK AT IT THIS WAY: Words can bring life or death and comments like these are mean-spirited. If a worshipper brings something like this to our attention we should be prepared to address their concern by saying something similar to this. "You obviously have no idea of what it means for Sister Odell and those beautiful praise dancers to praise God through song and dance. And for all you know Brother Roscoe may have written some of those wonderful tunes but just never got the credit for them. He should be encouraged and loved on too. If your comments were overheard they might prevent someone else from coming forth to participate in something that is absolutely awesome and wonderful? I believe God honors whatever service we present to Him in sincerity and love." Of course as with everything, use discernment and wisdom and always be mindful of how something is said.

SITUATION: <u>Craig the Critical</u>—*"Look at him. He's the minister and he should know better than to wear that ugly purple suit up in the pulpit. He looks like that dinosaur my grandkids watch on television. Last Sunday he had on a tie that was so loud I had to pull out my sunglasses to even look at him during his sermon. And who in the world taught him how to speak. He splits every verb in the dictionary. If you ask me I think he should take some English lessons along with learning how to dress."*

LOOK AT IT THIS WAY: Just because he is your minister does not mean he has your taste in clothing or your perceived grasp of the King's English. And what difference does that really matter if he is delivering the Word of God the way he has been instructed. If his taste in clothing is that much of a distraction I am sure he would not mind having some new ones from a few of his more dissatisfied members. Make every attempt to look past your personal dislikes when they have nothing to do with the real issues at hand and when you come into God's house be sure you understand what the real issues are.

ON THE OTHER HAND: As a minister or leader, who stands before others, be mindful to dress so that it is not an obvious distraction. Keep your individual sense of style but never wear anything that will speak louder than your word from God to His people. And if there is room for improvement in your delivery of the spoken word, consider taking a study course or getting a tutor to assist you.

In a Word...

How true is the description given about the tongue in James 3:6, "the tongue is a fire, a world of iniquity?" Have you ever been burned by that fire? It is a most unpleasant experience. Like a physical fire, the tongue can be a destroyer if uncontrolled. The good news is that God has given us the power to control our tongues if we are yielded to Him. We must remain conscious of the power of our words. There is life and death in the power of our tongue, choose to speak life.

PRAYER

Father God, keep me from evil thoughts and deeds. Help me to know my own frailties so that I will not be so quick to look at what I consider to be weaknesses or failures in others. Forgive me for having such a mean spirit and for speaking such ugly things about others especially when they are doing what is pleasing in your sight. I repent and I thank you for your patience and loving-kindness toward me.

NOTES

_____

_____

_____

_____

_____

_____

_____

_____

_____

_____

_____

_____

_____

_____

_____

_____

GIVE RESPECT WHERE RESPECT IS DUE

Those persons God has placed in our lives to equip us for the ministry, deserve nothing short of reverential awe and respect. Anything less could keep us from fully receiving what the Father has in store for us.

"And we beseech you, brethren, to know them which labor among you, and are over you in the Lord, and admonish you; And to esteem them very highly in love for their work's sake and be at peace among yourselves."
I Thessalonians 5:12-13

SITUATION: Friendly vs. common— *"Hey Rev, the main dog, how's it going?"*
LOOK AT IT THIS WAY: Now would this person say that to the President of the United States or to the Pope? Probably not because he understands the importance of giving them respect. Those persons ordained to this very important role deserve no less. Know the difference between being warm and friendly versus being too common. Learn how to respect those who have been called to these positions of authority. Imagine what a person still in the world would think after hearing a minister being addressed in a disrespectful way. How much respect would they be willing to give to the pastor and other church leaders? Do you think they would be willing to listen to and apply godly counsel from "Rev, the main dog?"

SITUATION: <u>Oh, it's only you</u>— *"Hi, Rev. Golden. I'm glad to see you this morning. You look exceptionally pretty in that dress and your message was great as usual." "Why thank you, Mr. Anderson. I appreciate the compliment. Now, I'm sure you didn't mean to overlook my handsome husband standing right here. In fact, could I get you to move over a bit? You're standing right between us and you know I don't let anything come between my beloved and me."*
LOOK AT IT THIS WAY: A+ for Rev. Golden! Although this worshipper may not necessarily have a romantic interest in her, it's good to let this man **and** her husband know that she will not allow anyone to disrespect her spouse. Of course it's important **how** this response is given. Many people don't mean to disrespect a spouse but when they see an opportunity to meet and greet a leader they get tunnel vision. Understand that in most cases, you can enjoy the message from your pastor because their spouse has helped to create an atmosphere conducive for just that. Give them their props as well.

In a Word...

Everyone deserves to be treated with respect and dignity. That respect shouldn't diminish as we become more familiar with a person. When we communicate with persons in positions of authority, protocol dictates that we add another layer of respect. It's not artificial or pretentious, but a sincere acknowledgment of the person's special calling and position. Such is the case with pastors, their spouses and others in Christian leadership. Let your attitude and behavior be appropriate to the position the person has been placed in. The Bible tells us to esteem those highly who are in service to the Lord. That esteem must translate to the language and actions directed to them.

PRAYER

*Lord, I want to fit in so badly and have my minister notice me.
Sometimes I don't know what to say, so I end up saying something
totally inappropriate. Forgive me also for those times I have either
knowingly or unknowingly overlooked my minister's spouse. I'm
beginning to understand the importance of respecting those over me.
Thank You for placing me in this body of believers.
I am truly blessed and I thank you.*

NOTES

_____

_____

_____

_____

_____

_____

_____

_____

_____

_____

_____

_____

_____

_____

_____

_____

_____

TEAMWORK

Most people join a ministry by either hopping into the first one that strikes their fancy, joining one that is campaigning for extra hands, or by taking the time to discover the ministry God has assigned them to. Ministries provide opportunities for us to learn and to fine-tune our gifts – all of which will result in bringing more souls to the Kingdom of God. In the process let's remember that God is the One that not only designs ministries, but He also desires that we work within His framework of those ministries.

"The heart of the prudent getteth knowledge;
and the ear of the wise seeketh knowledge."
Proverbs 18:15

"Do you see a man wise in his own eyes?
There is more hope for a fool than for him."
Proverbs 26:12

"There are different kinds of gifts, but the same Spirit. There are
different kinds of service, but the same Lord. There are different
kinds of working, but the same God works all of them in all men.
Now to each one the manifestation
of the Spirit is given for the common good."
I Corinthians 12:4-7

SITUATION: <u>Let the games begin</u> – *"I knew I would get Sunday school teacher of the year again. I made sure I had everything together so I could beat out all of the other teachers and get that honor for myself again this year."*
LOOK AT IT THIS WAY: He never mentioned his love for this ministry or his desire to see the students grow spiritually and he never said he would share with other teachers those things that *seem*

to make him so successful. This could very well be an example of what sounding brass or a clanging cymbal sounds like. It may **appear** that this teacher has all of his ducks in a row and is doing an excellent job of training his young charges. But because he is doing it all for the glory of man and not for the love of his students it actually profits him nothing. *"...Love does not parade itself, is not puffed up; does not behave rudely, does not seek its own..."*
I Corinthians 13:4; 5

SITUATION: <u>Ask anyway</u>— *"I know how to do this. I've done it before. We used to do the same thing at my old church."*
LOOK AT IT THIS WAY: Are you sure? This might be a little different. Just because something may look familiar does not mean it is the same as what you have done or experienced before. In fact, your actions could have some devastating effects on you and other members. Even though it may seem like a 'no-brainer' always ask so the outcome will be a desirable one.

SITUATION: <u>Name that tune</u>—*Woman singing:* ♫♫ *"I feel like going **home**, I feel like going **home**. When trials come on every hand, I feel like going **home**."* ♫♫ *The person next to her is singing:* ♫♫ *"I feel like going **on**, I feel like going **on**. When trials come on every hand, I feel like going **on**."* ♫♫
LOOK AT IT THIS WAY: The first version sounds like a depressed person considering suicide. The next version is a song of hope. Always find out the correct way to do anything once you discover that your way may not be the best. It can make a huge difference sometimes.

SITUATION: <u>Ministry mix-match</u>—*"I have a passion and an anointing when it comes to working with children...**Sit down little boy before I send you to your mother!** Oh yes, I just love working with God's little lambs. They're just precious. **You all had better stop making all that racket in here or I'll...**"*
LOOK AT IT THIS WAY: Now this person may have a passion and an anointing but not necessarily for children. Those adults who don't have the patience to work with these noisy little bundles of energy must reconsider this type of ministry. To offend one of these little ones is a sure fire way to sometimes offend the big ones they

belong to. Be honest with yourself and know what your passions really are. Don't force anything on yourself or on others that you know in your heart you won't enjoy being committed to.

SITUATION: <u>**How did you get "up" there so fast?**</u>—*"I've been a member of this church for 23 years and it took me 11 years to become a ministry leader. Dee just joined this church last year and Rev. Peeples chose her to become a leader after six months? That's just not right."*

LOOK AT IT THIS WAY: Matthew 20:1-16 speaks about the workers in the vineyard who each were hired and agreed to being paid one penny per day. But when the workers saw that those workers last hired got paid the same as those hired first; they became upset. Here's what the vineyard owner had to say: *"Friend I am doing you no wrong; did you not agree with me for a denarius." Take what is yours and go, but I wish to give to this last man the same as to you. Is it not lawful for me to do what I wish with what is my own? Or is your eye envious because I am generous? So the last shall be first, and the first last."*

Promotions and other good things come from God. How God chooses to dole out HIS blessings, HIS mercy, HIS grace and HIS promotions, to HIS children, HIS servants and HIS friends is entirely up to HIM.

In a Word...

Is there anything more impressive than a group of individual personalities who set aside their differences to work together like a well-oiled machine? This is only possible when members recognize and respect the gifts within every other member of the group. Likewise, we must recognize our own limitations and acknowledge our own motivations and attitudes. Never remain in a position where the grace of God no longer resides. Allow God to put you in that place where you can be your very best and a benefit to the group.

PRAYER

Father, I love serving in Your House but I can become a bit over zealous at times and this has negatively affected others. I want to know my gifts so I can be effectively positioned where You would have me. Help me to include others and remove from me the need and desire to have such a controlling spirit at times. I need to remember that I can be an effective leader by taking charge but not by taking over. Thank you for reminding me that good ideas come from You through us and that I am not the only vessel You have chosen to use.

NOTES

_____

_____

_____

_____

_____

_____

_____

_____

_____

_____

_____

_____

_____

_____

_____

_____

FAMILY SQUABBLES

Just because it's the church doesn't mean there won't be trouble between the brothers and sisters from time to time. Because we are children of the Most High He has provided us with the tools to get through the most difficult situations.

"Agree with thine adversary quickly, whiles thou art in the way with him; lest at any time the adversary deliver thee to the judge..."
Matthew 5:25

"Pursue peace with all people, and holiness without which no one will see the Lord; looking carefully lest anyone fall short of the grace of God; lest any root of bitterness spring up cause trouble, and by this many become defiled"
Hebrews 12:14-15

"...Yes, all of you be submissive to one another, and be clothed with humility, for God resists the proud but gives grace to the humble. Therefore humble yourselves under the mighty hand of God, that He may exalt you in due time."
I Peter 5:5-6

SITUATION: Lobbying— *"Cynthia, did you hear what Bianca and that committee did to me again? They're always rejecting my ideas. God gave me the anointing to do this and I have my degree in this same field. Half of the people on that committee read on a fifth grade level so what do they know and who do they think they are?"*
LOOK AT IT THIS WAY: This person is attempting to get Cynthia to side with him by pointing out what he considers to be an injustice. He expects that others will become upset too. Tell him and any other lobbyists that because God gave the gift He will also give

many opportunities to express it. Going around in an attempt to get others on this bandwagon is one of those things on God's hate list. (*Proverbs 6:16-19)* If an idea is rejected, remember it is generally nothing to be offended by. It may a good idea but the wrong time to implement it or this idea may not be a part of the vision for this particular church. Refrain from having "after the meeting *meetings*" if things do not go your way. Don't make negative comments about the person(s) whose views or opinions may be different from yours. Sit down one on one with that person in an attempt to better explain your position and to better understand theirs.

SITUATION: <u>Conflict and confrontation</u>—*"I've had it with all of you. I'm the only one who cares anything about this ministry. I seem to be the only one who makes all of the phone calls, types up the handouts and my house is the one used most of the time so I end up preparing most of the refreshments each month. This is ridiculous and I'm sick of listening to the rest of you just pray and sing."*

LOOK AT IT THIS WAY: This person sounds a lot like Martha who was busy serving but found no joy in it (*Luke 10:39-42).* She had allowed the work of the Lord to become more important than the Lord of the work. Attitudes like hers allow satan to rob us of our purpose within a ministry and cause us to focus only on ourselves. We only see how stressed and unappreciated we are. We can also rob others who would want to become a part of the ministry. No one would want to become associated with members whose attitudes reflect that of an overworked whiner.

ON THE OTHER HAND: If a member wrongly accuses others of not pulling his or her weight, they should simply apologize and promise to be more productive. Denying it could easily result in an escalated conflict which could cause leaders to get involved. Nip it in the bud while you can.

In a Word...

While we can't always avoid conflicts and confrontations, we can learn positive ways of handling them. The following is taken from:

The Word for You Today
by Bob Gass:

- *When difficult situations and conflicts arise make sure the issue you're dealing with is worth your time and energy.*
- *Don't become distracted by something insignificant. Look to see how Jesus handled the circumstances you are facing today.*
- *Don't destroy the other person's self confidence.*
- *Stay away from all-inclusive statements such as "you always" or "you never."*
- *Assure the person that you have confidence in them and their ability to recover and handle things better next time. After all, that's what God does with you.*
- *Correction will do much; encouragement will do much more.*
- *Deal with people on an individual basis. Comparisons can cause resentment.*
- *It's easier to be critical than creative, but unless you're willing to help you're not qualified to get involved!!*
- *Straighten out the problem, not the person.*
- *Leave the person with these three things:*
  (1) A clear understanding of the problem
  (2) The assurance of your love
  (3) Encouragement and confidence that they can turn it around and that you'll help them to do just that.

Avoiding confrontation means failing to use the tools God has given us to restore harmony. Confrontation is speaking the truth in a personal, face-to-face encounter with those we value. Speaking the truth in love means taking a risk. It requires two fundamental convictions. First: That honesty is more important than avoiding conflict. Second: That the other person's well being is more important than their comfort level. God lovingly confronts us in areas where we need to grow and He expects us to do the same with others.

- *Don't talk about them, talk to them.*
- *Provide examples without exaggeration, spiritual hype or a lot of emotion. Give specific examples. Don't hide behind "I believe the Lord has shown me that you are wrong."*
- *Allow enough time between the offense and the confrontation for a prayerful defusing of any anger you may feel.*
- *Show them a better way. Don't leave them without clear direction on how to improve. Your goal should be to help them, not to guilt trip them.*
- *Show compassion and understanding. Approach them with genuine love and concern.*
- *Be sure! Make certain you have a good reason to confront.*
- *Confrontation should be a rare event, not an everyday occurrence.*
- *You should not relish the experience. If you do, stop and examine your motives.*
- *Be sensitive. Every situation is different. Make sure your words and your tone fit the person you are dealing with. Keep your own personal agenda in check. None of this is about you.*

PRAYER

Lord, help me do those things You have given me to do without being overly concerned with the assignments of my brothers and sisters. Forgive me for the times I have stirred up strife in the church when things did not go my way. Lord, I want so badly to be recognized. Help me to stop looking to others for my recognition and to seek only Your approval. Father, help me to always remember that promotion comes from You. Give me strength, love and patience so that I will become one who is a willing servant filled with Your love.

NOTES

BODY LANGUAGE

Non-verbal communication is just as important as verbal. In fact it can speak a lot louder than the actual spoken word. Communicate so that you set a standard that will raise the standards of others.

> *"I will forget my complaint,*
> *I will put off my sad face and wear a smile."*
> *Job 9:27*

> *"Give instruction to a wise man, and he will be still wiser;*
> *Teach a just man, and he will increase in learning."*
> *Proverbs 9:9*

SITUATION: <u>I'm just trying to brighten up their day</u> — *Little Jamal was in church not being disruptive, loud or causing any kind of disturbance. He was only turning around and smiling and waving at everyone he saw. When his mom noticed what he was up to she pinched him hard on the arm and said, "Stop all of that grinning. You're in church." Little Jamal began to cry and his mom then said, "Now that's more like it."*
LOOK AT IT THIS WAY: How sad it is for Christians to think it is unspiritual to show joy. If a person needed cheering up would they select a group of sad sacks who looked as though they'd lost their only friend. We are children of the most-high King. That is reason enough to be joyful and to show it.

SITUATION: <u>Sour pickle with lemon, anyone?</u>—*"Mommy, that man always looks so mean and he never smiles at anyone. When the pastor tells a joke, that's when I really see him frown and look especially mad. Is he sick or something?"*
LOOK AT IT THIS WAY: A smile is universal and everyone can appreciate one especially when it's genuine. A smile can be warfare

and it can defeat a lot of what ails you and others. Remember that people cannot see what is in our hearts. They can only go by what is shown on the outside.

SITUATION: Why don't you smile? — *"Catherine, every time I see you, you've got the saddest expression. Why don't you smile more? You should see yourself."*
LOOK AT IT THIS WAY: Rather than demanding a smile from Catherine, why not give her a reason to smile more. Pay her a compliment; share something wonderful you may have found out about an accomplishment or hobby of hers. Maybe you can say something nice about her appearance. It doesn't take much. Besides we never know what Catherine or others may be going through. So why not brighten up their life for a few minutes. Everyone can find something good to say about another if a little effort is put into it.

SITUATION: Cooties? —*"I like Bruce but I think I must make him uncomfortable. Every time I greet him with a handshake he holds my hand like I've got the plague and he stands back about two feet when I try to hug him."*
LOOK AT IT THIS WAY: Assuming you have done a self-breath check, your hands don't look like the coal miner's daughter and you know you're giving holy hugs, maybe Bruce and others like him just aren't comfortable communicating non-verbally. Try using a little humor by saying you need a better hug or handshake from him than that. Non-verbal communication is just as important as verbal communicating. A person can be perceived as cold and unfriendly if they do not smile, give good eye contact, hugs and handshakes. Our behavior 'teaches' others, so we must use these kinds of situations as opportunities to show a more excellent way.

SITUATION: The language is all the same – *"I don't know sign language so I can't speak with those hearing impaired members. I don't even feel comfortable around them because I can't communicate with them."*
LOOK AT IT THIS WAY: Mark Twain said, "Kindness is the language which the deaf can hear and the blind can see." Everyone understands a smile and a hug. These are two of the best and most effective ways to communicate. So what if you don't know how to

sign. You could learn, but in the mean time, do what would make you feel good if you were that hearing impaired person. Take time to speak slowly and deliberately so that your lips can be read while giving big, warm holy hugs and a smile that could brighten up the darkest room.

In a Word...

Never underestimate the power of a smile, touch or gesture. Strong messages of acceptance, empathy or love are received without a word being spoken. On the other hand, a roll of the eyes, turn of the lips or wrinkle of the brow can negate any kind words that are offered. We must be aware of how we communicate messages to others through our body language. A limp handshake or a turn-aside from a kiss can cause a person to receive a negative vibe that brings his spirit down. Be sure that your body language communicates the positive message that brings a feeling of warmth and love.

PRAYER

*Father I thank You that I am comfortable with who I am in You.
Help me to be more tolerant of those in the Body who may be shy or
those unable to communicate verbally. Teach me to be more
effective in my non-verbal communicating so that those I am around
will feel Your love through me.*

NOTES

_____

_____

_____

_____

_____

_____

_____

_____

_____

_____

_____

_____

_____

_____

LEADERSHIP

There are many leaders within our churches who come only to receive, forgetting that the role of leader is that of a giver. We forget that these God-ordained appointments were created to give of what God has placed within us for the betterment of others. It's never good to assume any of us are in this place of influence only because of mere talent, gifts or experience. God has placed many of us "up" in this spotlight to be seen and examined by others. This should make us (as leaders) more mindful of the need to continuously examine our motives, behaviors and attitudes. This place of authority is where others can watch, learn and even sometimes imitate us, thus making us more aware of where many of our more challenging areas of leadership lie. In the end these experiences serve to burn the dross away from the gold that lies beneath.

"Give therefore thy servant an understanding heart to judge thy people, that I may discern between good and bad; for who is able to judge this thy so great a people?"
I Kings 3:9

"Listen to no accusation against an elder unless it is confirmed by the testimony of two or three witnesses."
I Timothy 5:19

"Is it not written, 'My house shall be called a house of prayer for all nations'? But you have made it a den of thieves."
Mark 11:17

SITUATION: I can handle everything without you— *"What's the point in her asking us for recommendations? She has never used any of them in the past and that is not likely to change. You know her favorite unspoken saying, 'It's my way or the highway'. I know* *there is a lot more in store for this ministry. I pray she will begin utilizing some of the talent here and listening to some of the wonderful suggestions that many of us have. But for now we won't continue complaining. We'll just keep her and our ministry in prayer."*

LOOK AT IT THIS WAY: One of the most important lessons leaders must learn is that whatever God gives will always involve other people. Good leaders should always be looking for ways to work themselves out of a job. When a leader has equipped and empowered his or her team, ideas will flow. If these ideas are in line with the vision and mission of that ministry, you've got a win-win situation; ideas that can be implemented to help move the ministry forward using loyal, committed members who know they are respected and a vital part of the planning. The scripture reference above in *Mark 11:17* speaks of robbing the house of God of its money. It also makes me think of robbing the house of God of another of its valuable resources. Those are the gifts and talents given by God to be used in His house. Many leaders in the church have robbed others of their joy, creativity, self-esteem and more. How? By not helping them to discover and develop their own gifts and talents and by not giving persons under their leadership the necessary encouragement and equipment to do even greater things. The house of God is robbed when leaders deliberately place or keep a person in a position that stagnates their growth and by leaders who become insecure when the greatness of one under their leadership begins to show. Saul began to hate David when he saw his gifts and popularity blossom. David could have taken the low road and done a great deal of harm to Saul, even killing him. But like David we too who are under Saul-like leadership must take the high road and duck when the javelins are being thrown while still moving toward the completion of our God-given assignments. Every leader must look to God who anoints and appoints. Take a look at *Exodus 31:1-6* *"Then the Lord spoke to Moses saying: See, I have called by name Bezalel the son of Uri, the son of Hur, of the tribe of Judah.* **(God told the leader, Moses, who He had specifically appointed)** *And I have filled him with the Spirit of God, in wisdom, in understanding, in knowledge, and in all manner of workmanship, to design artistic works, to work in gold, in silver, in bronze, in cutting jewels for setting in carving wood, and to work in all manner of* *workmanship.* **(God gave specific gifts to a specific man so that he could complete specific tasks.)** *And I, indeed I, have appointed with him Aholiab the son of Ahismach, of the tribe of Dan; and I have put wisdom in the hearts of all the gifted artisans, that they may make all that I have commanded you."* **(God then told Moses who He had chosen as his (Moses) associate/assistant. He shared how He had qualified others to help carry out the work Moses had been commanded to do.)** God will take a lot of the stress out of our leadership roles if we would only listen for His instructions.

SITUATION: <u>Ministry ownership</u> — *"I just joined the Kitchen Ministry but each time I go down to the kitchen to help I get ordered around and treated like an intruder. The leader keeps telling me that only two people know how to operate some of the more complicated kitchen equipment. Why can't I learn how to operate it too? I don't mind washing dishes and mopping the floor, but what's wrong with me using my cooking skills from time to time.*
LOOK AT IT THIS WAY: This is one of the fastest ways to run a person away. By not allowing other willing worshippers to become full partners in a ministry can sometimes lead them to become involved in other ministries not ordained of God. They may become frustrated pew warmers or just simply leave the church altogether. Being the current leader of a ministry does not mean you will always be the leader or even a part of that ministry. Keep your team members prepared to step in. What good is a ministry that must shut down, cancel or postpone everything because one or two people cannot show up? As a leader, you must find ways to include and empower each of your members in some capacity. No one or two people should be the only ones who have the information and know-how to keep a ministry moving. You are charged with sharing pertinent knowledge and information that will keep your team consistently prepared and motivated. This is how they will be ready to take on the role of leader in your absence or when God moves you to your next assignment.

SITUATION: <u>Just a *little* encouragement</u> -- **"***I know you're excited about the Christmas play. You did a fantastic job. I can't believe you wrote it and you're also going to direct it. What did Pastor Gordon say to you about it? I know he's proud of you*

especially since this is the first play our little church has ever done."
"Well, even though I feel pretty good about the play, I was still
hoping that he would have taken a moment to give me a few words
of encouragement or at least mention my name in last month's
newsletter."

LOOK AT IT THIS WAY: *"Take heed that you do not do your*
charitable deeds before men, to be seen by them. Otherwise you
have no reward from your Father in heaven. Therefore, when you
do a charitable deed, do not sound a trumpet before you as the
hypocrites do in the synagogues and in the streets, that they may
have glory from men. Assuredly, I say to you, they have their
reward. But when you do a charitable deed, do not let your left hand
know what your right hand is doing, that your charitable deed may
be in secret; and your Father who sees in secret will Himself reward
you openly." Matthew 6:1-4

ON THE OTHER HAND: An effort of some kind should always
be made to support those taking the lead in getting things done
within a ministry. Many leaders fail to take a mere 60 seconds to
call and say thank you or to offer a word of encouragement for a job
well done. A little encouragement can go a long way especially to
those who really need it.

SITUATION: <u>5, 10, 15...Do I hear 20, 25, 30 ?</u>—*Minister to his*
congregation: "Church, I'm so pleased to announce that Mr. Robert
Ian gave over $10,000 to pay for the new musical instruments and
Dr. David Page gave a whopping $25,000 last month to help pay for
the new organ. I know the rest of you aren't going to let them beat
you in giving to the church. Come on now! Take out those check
books and let's see if you can do even better.

LOOK AT THIS WAY: How wonderful it is to be able to give
toward the needs in the House of God. But what's your motivation?
It should be because of your obedience to God. You should never
give in order to hear your name called out by a church leader.
Neither should your generosity be motivated only to have your name
printed on a program with more zeros behind it than another church
member. That could very well become your reward. Competition is
not a bad thing but it certainly can taint what God intended if used
incorrectly. Leaders, be careful not to encourage competition when
it results in misdirected motives and intentions. God wants us to be

cheerful givers because we give out of obedience and love for Him; not because we give more than another. *"Let nothing be done through selfish ambition or conceit; but in lowliness of mind let each esteem others better than himself. Let each of you look out not only for his own interests, but also for the interests of others."* Philippians 2:3-4

SITUATION: <u>Baptism by fire</u>— *"Church, we need six new Sunday school teachers. Can I get a show of hands of those who are interested? (Six people raise their hands.) This is great! After service today you each can pick up your teaching materials and on next Sunday I'd like you to meet your students and begin teaching your classes at 9am."*
LOOK AT IT THIS WAY: *Ephesians 4:11-12 says, "And Christ Himself gave some to be apostles, some prophets, some evangelists, and some pastors and teachers, for the equipping of the saints for the work of ministry for the edifying of the body of Christ."* Equipping means making ready for service and ministry. How can these wonderful servants equip others when they have not been adequately equipped themselves? Every church should have a process in place to effectively train those placed in a role where they can influence the thoughts and decisions of others. Attempt to find people who have had church or non-church experiences that will compliment what is needed. But remember they still may need to be retrained to do it according to a particular church's standard. Provide a job description. Clarify everything that is expected and required along with the implementation of a good **continuous** leadership improvement plan. Don't forget to offer refresher training as needed. Now the saints will be equipped to equip.

SITUATION: <u>I've got more important things to do</u> —*"Mother, I want you to meet one of our church leaders, Mrs. Marshall. You'll like her. She is such a sweet person. Mrs. Marshall, I want you to meet my Mom who is visiting from…"* *"Well dear, it looked as though your sweet Mrs. Marshall was much too busy to be bothered. She didn't even look this way and I know she heard you."*
LOOK AT IT THIS WAY: This is so embarrassing and it can make for some hurt feelings too. As a leader we should be aware of how others are sometimes drawn to us. Be mindful of this when

walking through crowds or entering a room. No church leader needs to be thought of as a snob or an uncaring person who is too busy to acknowledge others. This too is part of the territory.

SITUATION: Just bless us anyhow! – *"Last month the minister at St. John's asked me to conduct a two-day seminar. It took me almost three years to put this curriculum in place and with the handouts and other things it can be a bit costly to present. He told me that I would get paid but after the seminar he said my payment would be a continuous prayer from him. Oh yeah, he also said he'd be sure to have his associate ministers pray too. That would be my tip.*
LOOK AT IT THIS WAY: Obviously, this leader is not one of the great men the scripture says your gift will bring you before. (Proverbs 18:16) Why is it that some expect to receive payment for what they do but when it comes to paying for the gifts, skills and talents of others, it's a totally different story? Leaders sometimes want a person to forgo what is needed to cover their expenses in exchange for a fruit basket, a chicken dinner, a (questionable) prophecy or a prayer. And when did prayer come with a price tag and how can you even pay someone with prayer? Prayer is free! A check is a much better solution for payment. If you are unable to pay for a service, good stewardship suggests that you are honest upfront. Make payment arrangements. It is disrespectful to expect people to "bless you" at the expense of their livelihood. If they want to "bless you" allow that to be their choice because if your blessing is causing financial hardship for others, something is wrong with that picture.

SITUATION: Have you heard the whole story? – *"Lately Rev. Allen and some of our assistant ministers have been giving me the cold shoulder. I have prayed about this and asked God to show me what I may have done to them but I still don't have a clue. I'd like to ask them what may have happened but I just don't want to seem paranoid. Rev. Allen even had the church secretary to call and tell me that there would be no need for me to continue as a ministry leader. I've called several times in an attempt to speak to him but he is never available. I wish we could have had a conference of some kind so the entire situation could have been discussed. I thought I was doing a good job".*
LOOK AT IT THIS WAY: There aren't many good excuses or

reasons for church leaders to make important decisions without speaking to the person that decision will directly affect. This is especially true if a leader has received information which results in a termination, demotion or derogatory comments being made about a person. A fatal mistake some leaders make is to rely on unreliable information from unreliable sources; mere rumors or gossip. How dangerous is that? Leaders should always be willing and able to speak directly with the "accused" in an attempt to get a clearer and hopefully more accurate picture of a particular situation. The person bringing the information could very well be telling the truth but they could also be someone with an envious spirit, willing to do whatever it takes to bring about the fall of one they feel stands in their way. Here's something else to consider. Leaders along with their associates must never fall prey to a common playground tactic quite often used by young children. When a child is angry with some of her playmates, she may tell all of the other kids on the playground not to play with those children **she** is upset with. Of course little ones may go along with this practice if the little girl requesting the silent treatment is someone they all respect and look up to. It makes for an even worse situation when the ones being given the silent treatment don't even know *that* or *how* they have offended the little girl. Leaders, put away childish ways and stay in constant prayer for greater discernment, wisdom and love for those you lead just as Solomon did.

In a Word...

Being a church leader means being held to a higher standard. Your actions have the potential to affect many people without your even being aware. Because others watch you and often view you as a role model, you must be aware of the way you are perceived. Never allow your actions to cause someone else to stumble. Remember you are not just called to lead, but you are called to motivate, inspire and be a positive example to others.

PRAYER

God, it is pride that has caused me to offend others. Keep me from thinking I am too important to acknowledge others and remind me of what a true servant of God looks like. Forgive me for those times I have caused others pain because I did not use wisdom. I thank you for placing me in a leadership position. You trust me and I am honored. Help me to honor You by being a leader who shows a caring and loving attitude toward those under my leadership.

NOTES

WELCOME

As a church usher or greeter you must know your assignment. Not just where you should be physically positioned but you must know what is required of you as a door keeper of the Lord. Be proud of what you do and remember that an ounce of kindness can sometimes be worth more than a pound of preaching!

"Let us stop passing judgment on one another."
Romans 14:13

"And now I will show you the most excellent way."
I Corinthians 12:31

SITUATION: <u>Greeters and Ushers</u> — *An usher is attempting to show several worshipers where to sit by simply pointing to an available pew without any type of greeting or positive body language. A greeter nearby is busy chatting with fellow team members while handing out programs to entering worshipers. No eye contact or smiles are even being given because this greeter does not want to dis-engage from his/her conversation.*

LOOK AT IT THIS WAY: Ushers and greeters are often the first official representatives of Jesus Christ seen by people who enter God's house. If their job is to simply pass out programs, take up the offering or to stand and point to available pews, the church leaders could have easily trained a chimpanzee to fill that position. Being an usher or greeter means being a part of a ministry that was put in place to bring order. It also means being a part of a ministry that offers **visible** human love and kindness. Effective body language is crucial. These are the people that can set the tone for everything else to come within the worship service. Their attitudes can enhance or detract, contribute or contaminate the worship atmosphere simply by the way their duties are carried out. These door keepers of the Lord may be the only individual contact the church directly makes with a person during the worship service. Worshipers may not get an opportunity to talk to the pastor or to anyone on the ministerial staff. They may never even see a Sunday school teacher but they will in most cases always come in contact with an usher or a greeter.

In a Word...

Here are some additional tools every greeter and usher should consider:

- *Make every attempt to smile and maintain a warm and sincere countenance.*
- *Bend over backwards and give more than is expected even when worshipers are acting 'un-Christian'. Do it genuinely with a good attitude; not sarcastically or half heartedly.*
- *When members or visitors need your assistance to find classes, restrooms etc, never just point to the general vicinity. Instead "take them" to where they need to be. If you cannot personally accompany these worshipers, always* **lovingly** *pass them to another who can.*
- *All problems encountered by greeters and ushers cannot be solved right away or to a person's satisfaction but every attempt must be made to do so with wisdom and love.*
- *If you cannot solve an irate worshiper's problem or concern right away attempt to get their name and contact information. Apologize for not being able to solve the problem immediately but let them know you will make every effort to get an answer, solution, explanation etc. within a specific time frame. i.e.*
- *Follow up and follow through!!*
- *Show the value of following rules that are in place by telling worshipers the reason(s) why the rule was made.*
- *Use common sense and wisdom when attempting to get a worshiper to follow a rule. Never force someone to follow a rule when your doing so will distract from the service.*
- *Maintain order but learn to let some things go. It's just not worth it in some cases. The "you're going to follow this rule we came up with or else" attitude will not always work.*
- *Never make worshipers feel like they will burn in hell for not following a rule that the usher board came up with.*

PRAYER

Lord, I pray that I will fulfill my assignment as a doorkeeper of the Lord in a Christ-like way. Make me efficient in what I do, effective in what I say, understanding by the way I feel about people, and helpful in the attitudes I have toward them. Make me a coworker with the pastor, the church musicians, the teachers and most of all, Lord with You.

Save me from hurtful words and harmful deeds. Help me to wrap every word and clothe every action in the spirit of human kindness. Let my kind of Christianity help people to let down their guards, open their hearts, and relax their minds for the worship of God and direction of His Holy Spirit.

Help me to be understanding with the difficult people and to exercise compassion with all kinds of people, to be efficient but not at the expense of kindness.

Help me to assist in setting and maintaining an atmosphere that will make people glad they came to our church because the Holy Spirit ministered to their needs through the sermons and prayers of the pastor, through the songs of the musicians, through the knowledge of the teachers, and through the ministry of ushers like me.

Parts of this prayer were taken from
"Serving as a Church Usher"
By Leslie Parrott,
Zondervan Practical Ministry Guides

NOTES

LAZYBONES

What happens when Christians give only a portion of what is actually required of them? Not much! In fact we end up leaving a trail of confusion and many souls lost because of our half-hearted efforts to get the things of God accomplished.

"The lazy man will not plow because of winter;
He will beg during harvest and have nothing."
Proverbs 20:4

"Without counsel, plans go awry,
but in the multitude of counselors they are established."
Proverbs 15:22

SITUATION: <u>Ten-toed sloth</u> --*"Come and join the Hostess Ministry with me. It's so much fun. You get a chance to see everybody and everybody gets a chance to see you in your cute little uniform. Oh, don't worry about serving every month. They have over 100 people in our ministry so if you don't feel like serving when it's your turn, no problem. Somebody is always there to fill in for you. You'll love it!"*

LOOK AT IT THIS WAY: How dare you join a ministry and give only a piece of what you really have to offer and a tainted piece at that! When you join any kind of organization, people expect you to be committed. They are counting on you to be in place exactly as you said you would be and they expect you to do whatever task that particular ministry requires. If you want to become a part of a ministry, know what its mission and duties are. If they don't line up with what you can or want to handle, keep praying and looking until you find the one that does.

SITUATION: <u>Are we ready yet?</u> —*"Wow, it's 11:25 and the 11:00 service still hasn't started. This has happened several times within the last few weeks. And what's happening with the choir? I know there are about 75 members but only about 25 show up to sing each Sunday. What is going on?"*

LOOK AT IT THIS WAY: For church services, ministry meetings, etc., God requires a spirit of excellence, which includes promptness, loyalty, and commitment. Nothing we do for God should be done with a lackadaisical attitude. People who so desperately need the Word should never be kept waiting to receive it. Church leaders must hire and or appoint those persons who are willing to do whatever it takes to ensure all is done in decency and in order. There can be no exceptions.

SITUATION: <u>So great a sacrifice?</u>—*"Our church has grown so fast that we have run out of parking space. I had to park at a school and take the shuttle to the church. The bus filled up so quickly I had to stand up. I just knew one of the men would let me have their seat. But do you know that there was not one single man (deacons and ministry leaders included) willing to give up their seat to me or to any of the other women who were standing."*

LOOK AT IT THIS WAY: Chivalry must not die in the house of God. Men, remember that young boys are always watching you with many of them wanting to be just like you. This is a time to shine and show them the actions of a true man of God. Every now and then we all get tired and want to sit in a comfortable seat. Rosa Parks certainly knew how that felt. And moms, this is a perfect opportunity to teach your young sons and daughters how to acknowledge women and the elderly by offering their seats with a good attitude and a smile.

ON THE OTHER HAND: Ladies, remember it's perfectly all right to offer **your** seats to the elderly and to those men and women (i.e. ushers and greeters) who have been standing on their feet during most of the church service.

SITUATION: A call unanswered—*"I really need some help with this project. I was told to call Ethel if I had any problems but it has been over three weeks and she has not returned any of my calls or e-mails. I wonder if I should just make a decision on my own or just forget about this project altogether."*

LOOK AT IT THIS WAY: Leaders or others in charge should never leave a person stranded. Give clear directions regarding a task and be prepared to provide other resources in the event you are unavailable so the work can proceed. If you find that you never have opportunities to return calls or e-mails, you may need to take a long hard look at how you are prioritizing your day and managing your time and energy. People who are much busier than you find time to return calls and e-mails. One callback can take as little as two minutes or less especially when you let the person know why you are calling and advise them that you cannot spend a lot of time on the call because of other demands. If you're afraid you'll get snagged into a long drawn out conversation send an e-mail or use snail-mail. Don't forget to apologize for not calling back sooner.

In a Word...

When you accept the responsibility of service in your church, realize that you have a commitment to meet the needs of the ministry. The same work ethic you bring to your place of employment should be applied to your ministry service. After all you are serving others as unto the Lord. Sometimes it may mean serving when you'd rather not; it's the nature of sacrifice. When we give half-hearted service, we show a lack of maturity and a blatant disrespect for the work of the kingdom. Give your service in a way that brings honor to God.

PRAYER

Lord, I thank you for the opportunity to serve. Help me to learn how to better manage my time and energy so that I will be a more effective servant. I will no longer take Your people for granted by repeatedly being late and not being in place for them. Forgive me for not prioritizing my day to get those assignments completed that have been given by You. Order my steps each day and help me to listen for Your precious Holy Spirit who will guide and direct me to get things done.

NOTES

_____

_____

_____

_____

_____

_____

_____

_____

_____

_____

_____

_____

_____

_____

_____

_____

MONEY ISSUES

Because of unemployment, over extended budgets, bad habits and just plain old hard times many churches today are laden with money problems from borrowers and thieves. We've got to remember that many will come to the House of God not for the Word but to see what they can get from those who do come for the Word.

"You shalt not steal."
Exodus 20:15

"Wealth gained by dishonesty will be diminished,
but he who gathers by labor will increase."
Proverbs 13:11

"The rich rules over the poor,
and the borrower is servant to the lender."
Proverbs 22:7

SITUATION: <u>Stealing in the name of the Lord</u>—*"Oh, I just found $50 in the men's room. Thank you, God. You do supply all my needs".*
LOOK AT IT THIS WAY: Thou shall not steal applies in and out of church. Don't pick up things that don't belong to you and think you just got blessed. Do the right thing. Take it to a minister, another leader or to the lost and found.

SITUATION: <u>The haves and the have-nots</u>— *"They can afford it. They will hardly miss this little bit of money I'm **borrowing**. This church has over $5 million dollars worth of cars in the parking lot and the minister drives a car worth more than my house. Anyway, I heard that some of these people do some questionable things in order to live so well. Besides, didn't I hear the pastor say 'the poor you'll always have with you?' What do they expect?"*

LOOK AT IT THIS WAY: The Word also says that there is a consequence for every action-good and bad. Wouldn't it be a wiser decision to ask for help rather than to help yourself to what is not yours for the taking. No one wants to be the victim of theft especially when they have worked hard to do what was required of them in order to have the blessings of the Lord. Even if those items were gotten in a questionable way it is still left up to God to handle it. The scripture "...*But the wealth of the sinner is stored up for the righteous" (Proverbs 13:22)* does not mean we are to decide who the wealthy sinners are and to take from them. Besides, even if Robin Hood was a biblical character it could prove dangerous to follow in his footsteps.

SITUATION: <u>The human bank</u>—*"Cheryl, I really appreciate you loaning me that $100 last week. I hate to ask again, but my little Babs sure could use some new shoes. You've got such a good heart and you know what I'm going through as a single parent."*
LOOK AT IT THIS WAY: Here is Cheryl's response. "I'm glad you appreciate the loan but we need to discuss a repayment plan because I'll need that back soon. Now about Babs' new shoes; I won't be able to help you with that. So let's look at that repayment plan." No one died and left Cheryl a bank. No matter how well off or generous a person is, no one should take advantage of another by repeatedly borrowing and sometimes not planning to ever repay the loan just because that person appears to be a well-to-do-church-going-Christian. Remember also that you should never loan anything you cannot afford to lose or that you may want back. If you're going to give money, give it don't loan it.

SITUATION: <u>Charity begins with me</u>— *"I'm broke again and I just got paid last week. I guess I should have thought twice about buying those three suits and eating out every day last week because my rent and car note are due next week. Oh well, I'll just let the church know so they can provide me **again** with another one of those benevolence checks. In the mean time I'm going to run on down to Macy's One Day Sale."*
LOOK AT IT THIS WAY: Churches have a benevolence fund for those persons who are in need. It is generally set aside for people who have run into an emergency situation or for those who need a

helping hand to get on their feet. It is not for those who **need** to look harder and smarter for a job or a better career. It is not for those who **need** to learn better budgeting and spending habits. It is not for those who **need** to stop relying solely and repeatedly on the church for their total survival. And it is definitely not for those who **need** to stop purchasing everything they *want* while relying on others for everything that they *need* such as housing, utilities, food, child care, etc. As members of the Body of Christ we must become more mature and much more disciplined when it comes to handling our finances. Most churches do not have a perpetual stream of money that they can continue to disperse to repeat borrowers. Remember too that what *you* continuously borrow from the church **cannot** then go to those parents who were burned out of their home and are struggling to feed their three small children or to that elderly person who has no funds to pay for much needed medicine and it cannot then go to that college senior who has been on his own and worked his way through school, but now needs money for this last semester. Something to consider…

SITUATION: <u>**Looking for your harvest in all the wrong**</u> <u>**places**</u>— *"Melba just got blessed with $10,000 and she only gave me a measly $1500. I can't believe she is so selfish after all I have done for her and her family throughout the years."*
LOOK AT IT THIS WAY: But if you didn't *loan* her any money you shouldn't expect her to repay you. Be thankful that she thought enough of you to share a part of her blessing with you. And if you were following God's instructions by helping this person in the past, God will determine how you will be repaid and He will make sure you are blessed accordingly. Too many Christians give and expect the recipient of our gift to bless us back in the same or a similar way. It doesn't necessarily work like that in God's kingdom. When people are blessed financially, don't spend so much time concentrating on THEIR blessing. In many cases that is merely their seed to move their God given vision further along. You probably have no idea what visions and dreams God has put in their heart and you certainly do not know the other financial obligations this person may have. Pulling out your calculator in an attempt to figure out what part of another's blessing should/could come to you will only result in disappointment and strained relationships. Don't be "the

hindrance" by pressuring someone to give you what could very well belong to God. *"You were running well; who hindered you from obeying the truth? This persuasion did not come from Him who calls you." Galatians 5:7-8*

In a Word...

Libraries of books have been written about the problems caused by unhealthy attitudes toward money. Many friendships and marriages are destroyed because of issues related to money. Often these concerns surface in the church. There are certain principles worth considering as you manage situations related to money in the church:

- Never loan what you can't afford to give.
- Never co-sign under any circumstance.
- Return whatever you borrow promptly.
- Respect what belongs to someone else. If you find it, realize somebody else lost it. You are not blessed at another person's expense.
- Always maintain integrity even when you're going through financial challenges.
- When the church provides you with money, it is for *basic* living expenses. It is not for all of the "extras" you may want but not need.
- Make it a habit *never* to share your financial matters with others especially when it is not necessary to do so.
- Many churches require members requesting financial assistance to provide personal documentation such as bank statements, bills, etc. Leaders should **never** discuss this information with others who have nothing to do with the decision to give a member aid. This includes other church members, leaders, administrators, outside coworkers, spouses and family members.

PRAYER

Lord, I am sorry. I am wrong to take what is not mine and to continuously borrow from others. I need so much for my family and myself but I also need to know how to better use the resources you have already provided for me. Help me to become more disciplined and to develop a greater desire to know Your Word and to follow Your laws. It is my impatience that has always caused me such pain and caused me to take from others. Help me to use wisely all that you will bring to me as I continue to seek Your will for my life.

NOTES

_____

_____

_____

_____

_____

_____

_____

_____

_____

_____

_____

_____

_____

_____

_____

_____

_____

_____

ARROGANCE, JUDGEMENT, PRIDE AND PREDJUDICE

A little bit of knowledge is a dangerous thing especially when it's mixed with judgmental attitudes and prideful spirits.

"Or did the word of God come originally from you?
Or was it you only that it reached?"
I Corinthians 14:36

"If anyone ministers, let him do it as with the ability which
God supplies, that in all things God may be glorified through
Jesus Christ, to whom belong the glory and dominion
forever and ever, Amen."
I Peter 4:11

"So then, they are no longer two but one flesh. Therefore what God
has joined together, let not man separate."
Matthew 19:6

SITUATION: <u>Spiritual arrogance</u>— *"I can't believe he is so stupid. He should have at least known what the first five books of the Bible are called. Everybody knows that."*
LOOK AT IT THIS WAY: You didn't come out of the womb preaching and quoting scriptures, so why would you look down on someone who hasn't studied or heard as much Word as you have. You are in that Bible study to learn what you don't know and to humbly and lovingly teach what you have learned. We should never come to merely pontificate in an attempt to impress some while intimidating others. Remember, you are adding no jewels to your crown by running someone off who is hungry for the Word.

SITUATION: <u>Snobs and snubs</u>— *"Gail and Loretta, didn't I tell you both to stop hanging around that horrible looking little girl. Her family may come to church every now and then but they look like heathens. I don't ever want anyone to see either of you with a person who looks like that."*

LOOK AT IT THIS WAY: What kind of message are these young people receiving from their parents? They are being taught to love like Jesus loved but to separate themselves from another because of how that person looks. They will certainly be confused. No one, especially children, should be sent mixed messages regarding the teachings of Christ. Adults must always set the example and teach children to do the same. We must all show how to walk out the true love of Christ.

SITUATION: <u>Parking lot preachers</u>—*"That message was right on time for me. I had been praying for an answer to a problem and Rev. Benjamin's message has really helped me figure this thing out." "Yeah, yeah that might be one way to look at it but you've got to understand what he was really trying to say to you was..."*

LOOK AT IT THIS WAY: Don't you love it when others don't ask but will assume you didn't understand the message so they feel the need to 'break it down' for you? Lovingly remind these pulpit wannabes that you appreciate their input and you will prayerfully consider it; but right now you want to meditate on what you know was laid on your heart.

SITUATION: <u>The litmus test</u>— *"I can understand needing a place to live, but no righteous Christian should have a need or desire to live in a big expensive house like theirs. That car they drive must have cost a fortune. And have you seen those expensive clothes their children wear? The church could do a lot with the kind of money they're wasting. They should consider living in a more humble way because all this showy stuff is definitely not of God."*

LOOK AT IT THIS WAY: Is it right to judge another's level of spirituality based on the type of home, car or clothing they have? All of what you see could be gifts from a loving relative or friend. Or they just may be financially able to afford all of it along with regularly paying their tithes, offerings, alms and other giving. In either case, no one who is financially well off (while looking the part) should be subjected to an investigation of their spirituality. Why wouldn't God want His children to prosper and enjoy the fruits of their labor? That's a testimony in itself.

SITUATION: The un-match-maker—*"I know I'm in church but I don't care if they do see me staring. I believe people should marry within their own race. They've got to know all of the problems they are creating especially for those kids. Why didn't they find someone to marry that looks like them? At least it would have been someone they could identify with. This hopping all over the rainbow is ridiculous."*

LOOK AT IT THIS WAY: Why not use that same energy to pray for those unions that come under such scrutiny and attack. Pray that adversity will make them stronger and draw them even closer to each other and to God. Be sure to pray for those who feel that God has not sanctioned these unions. Pray that those who feel this way will learn to bless what belongs to another so that God will bless them with wonderful relationships of their own.

In a Word...

A very ugly spirit has crept into the church when members display judgmental attitudes, arrogance, pride or prejudice. Jesus strongly rebuked those who manifested these attitudes. When we come across as self-righteous, overbearing or proud we create a negative atmosphere that is not conducive for others to be blessed. In reality, it can cause others to be hurt, offended and possibly separated from God. Also, you are doing nothing for your own relationship with God. Jesus made a point of displaying compassion and understanding wherever He went. As a follower, that should be your goal.

PRAYER

Lord, help me to remember that I don't know it all and others have a lot to contribute also. Forgive me for my judgmental, arrogant, prideful and prejudice spirit. Humble me so that I will be more of a blessing to others. I will listen more and talk less in order to learn and discern more from other vessels in the Body.

NOTES

PARTIALITY

Most of us love to shine and be in the spotlight. We also like to see our loved ones and those we admire being given special attention. Nothing is wrong with either as long as it is not at the expense of another.

"To show partiality is not good because for a piece of bread a man will transgress"
Proverbs 28:21

"But if you show partiality, you commit sin and are convicted by the law as transgressors.
"For whoever shall keep the whole law, and yet stumble in one point, he is guilty of all."
James 2:9-10

SITUATION: <u>Nepotism</u>— *"Wow, this is the third time in six months that the minister has asked his sister to facilitate our monthly leadership workshop. It would be great if some of our own members could get an opportunity to share their gifts along with the opportunity to earn that kind of income."*

LOOK AT IT THIS WAY: This is perfectly acceptable if the decision to use the Reverend's sister so often is a request from God. It's also acceptable if she is providing something that no one else is capable of. Leaders must be very careful not to overlook others within their very own ministry whose gifts need to be developed and stretched and who could also benefit financially from these opportunities.

ON THE OTHER HAND: Even if a decision seems a bit biased we still do not know what God has in mind. If this particular decision is of God, be patient. Your time is coming. Remember,

God is sovereign. He will harden a heart and close a door just to keep you from going where He is not quite ready for you to be. *"Paul and Silas...having been **forbidden by the Holy Spirit** to proclaim the Word in Asia. Acts 16:6* When your time comes many will be blessed and you will be able to give Him all of the glory.

SITUATION: <u>Favoritism</u> – *"Miss Brown, make sure you give Deacon Bell's son an extra helping of that apple pie. That's his favorite."*
LOOK AT IT THIS WAY: Go right ahead and give him that extra piece as long as the other children standing around watching don't mind. Of course that is quite unlikely even if they are as full as ticks. No child should be subjected to a feeling of 'not as good' because adults feel a need to acquire points with the parents of the so-called special children. How would you feel (as a child) if you got ignored while someone else got the royal treatment while you were only allowed to look on?

SITUATION: <u>"Mommy Dearest"</u>—*"I know Mrs. Ray's son has had the lead role in the Easter pageant each year. But what can we do? After all, he is the Sunday School Superintendent's child and she has made it clear that she wants him in that leading role every year."*
LOOK AT IT THIS WAY: It's wonderful to think of those you love as special but that doesn't mean you should expect everyone else to feel the same way because of **your** leadership role. Suppose there are others who are willing and capable of doing those same things that could also put them in the spotlight.
Church leaders must realize the message they may be sending by excluding and ignoring the gifts and talents of others. Every child (old and young) that is a child of the King is special and deserving of an occasional spotlight.

SITUATION:<u>Celebrity worshippers</u>—*"Isn't that Penny, the actress from that new television show? I don't think she has a hymnbook. Let me hop over this pew and give her mine. I might as well ask for an autograph while I'm there."*
LOOK AT IT THIS WAY: She came to worship and so did you. In the house of God everyone is a worshipper and no one should be

singled out with extra attention because of her status or position. Neither should they be harassed by possible groupies. Come to church prepared to assist and respect anyone who is in need—not just the rich and famous.

In a Word...

A natural tendency exists for people to want to identify or at least rub shoulders with someone of celebrity status or connection. But that is no justification for making a distinction between people. Showing partiality because of a person's money, degree, celebrity or position is always wrong. Can you imagine what others feel when they are sidelined because of this preferential treatment? All of us are creations of a sovereign God who makes no distinctions.

PRAYER

Father, forgive me when I have forced others to give my loved ones special attention. I have also deliberately overlooked the gifts of those within this very ministry after hearing Your Holy Spirit's direction to utilize them. Please forgive me for having my own agenda while ignoring Yours. Help me to stop disrespecting others while assisting some as a means to only draw attention to myself. I ask you to heal and soothe any wounds that I have caused as a result of ignoring the gifts and needs of others.

NOTES

_____

_____

_____

_____

_____

_____

_____

_____

_____

_____

_____

_____

_____

_____

_____

_____

_____

A FINAL WORD

Good customer service in any type of organization is what I like to think of as *a ministry of kindness.* It is what helps us effectively apply the Word of God to manage and lessen those offenses that are certain to come to us and that we are certain to bring to others. It is what keeps a customer coming back through the doors of any kind of business or organization. It knows how to address a customer's spoken or unspoken questions and concerns without apathy, coldness, condescension, gossiping or judgment.

How a business or church treats it's internal and external customers has a direct bearing on its profitability and expansion. The church has been called to expand the Kingdom of God by winning souls to Christ. The physical church is where we're taught Kingdom principles and where we learn how to become the walking-breathing-spiritual church. But as that spiritual church we cannot misrepresent Jesus by our less than favorable attitudes and expect the world to want what we have. An organization is destined for failure whose customers no longer see any value in doing business or maintaining a relationship there.

As the church we are called to set the standard in order to raise the standards of others. People look to us to set the pace and the example. But our humanness at times will not allow us to look past another's faults, their lack of experience or spiritual immaturity.

We fail to remember that people come to church carrying all of their expectations, frailties, habits and experiences. Of course, we cannot always anticipate how any of these will manifest or how we may affect them. But we have to be sensitive to these influences in people's lives and become more deliberate in our own attitudes and behaviors.

How we come across can make for a pleasant experience or one that completely destroys another person's desire to be a part of an organized or any other type of Christian worship experience.

We must never forget that we have the capacity to shape a person's attitude and even their future by what they may witness in **our** behavior and attitude. What others see in us can either drive them *from* or draw them *to* their designated place of worship.

Many have been driven away from the very church where God has placed them without having been uplifted, motivated, encouraged, empowered or educated. In many cases, through our insensitivity and lack of discernment we as Christians have caused a considerable amount of pain to our brothers and sisters. Church pain can be one of the worst pains anyone can experience.

Remember that whoever God sends into our places of worship should (at some point) feel like they have made the right choice by being there; that they are in the right place at the right time. This is one of the surest ways to introduce the world to our Lord and further populate the Kingdom.

When the Body of Christ is doing its job effectively, we will begin to see multitudes of people within our church walls and beyond. They will come with all of their emotional, physical, financial and spiritual life issues because they will understand that the church is where the broken become mended and made whole.

The masses will then recognize the church as a mature body of believers. They will acknowledge the true reign of Christ in His Church because we as His Body will no longer major in the minor and seek our own versions of righteousness. Christ will be recognized (in us) as we walk in the power of Kingdom love; remembering what we used to be like and what we still need to work on, giving even when no one says thanks, forgiving when others won't forgive us in return, coming early, staying late and giving everything we've got, even when no one notices.

We will then know without a doubt that we are the answers to our own prayers for unity and cooperative spirits within the Body of Christ. God will use us and He will begin the work for unity and cooperative spirits with us. We will come into the house of God prayed up and ready to extend love with our discernment in tact. Then and only then can we effectively and lovingly teach what we are taught, give what we are given and become a blessing to all of those God sends our way.

A FINAL PRAYER

Gracious God,
I thank You for allowing me to
complete this phase of my assignment.
I pray that all who have read this book will now have a
greater awareness of the attitudes
and behaviors that are brought into Your house.
Help us to understand and assume our responsibility to others who
are seeking spiritual growth within and outside of the church.
Bless every reader and give each of us a new perspective of what it
means to be in Your Kingdom, to win souls for Christ and to set
the standard for others to follow.
I pray that we will never forget that we are the Church and nothing
shall prevail against us that would hinder the work You have for us
to do.

In the mighty name of Jesus,
Amen

Workshops Include:

"Set the Standard"

Sessions vary from a two-hour to a two-day workshop
An examination of the attitudes, behaviors and work habits brought
into the workplace that affect our business customers, employers,
coworkers and home life

- Life Skills
- Employment Readiness
- Customer Service
- Effective Communication
- Office Politics
- Business Etiquette
- Leadership
- Mystery shoppers utilized to ascertain level of comprehension and training effectiveness

"Discovering My Greatness"

Sessions vary from a two-hour workshop to a two-week camp
An entrepreneurial curriculum designed for teens and adults which
teaches the components of successful business ownership,
career and character development

- Creating Business Opportunities
- Business Plan Design and Implementation
- Working for Others before Owning Your Own
- Setting the Standard in Customer Service
- Leadership
- Mistakes and Failures Redefined
- Budgeting, Saving and Investing
- Business and Social Etiquette
- Philanthropy and Mentorship

"Customer Service in God's House"

Sessions vary from two to three hours
Scriptural based, interactive workshop which examines the type of
customer service church goers give to each other
and to those in search of a church home and spiritual support

- Identifies and addresses the attitudes and behaviors worshippers bring that may prevent a person in need of spiritual support from ever coming or wanting to return to a particular place of worship.
- Compares level of service received in the business world to the service received within the church
- Special component created for ushers and greeters.
- *Mystery Worshippers* utilized to identify improvements or challenges within a congregation after workshop completion

"Children, Our Ultimate Customer"

Sessions vary from two to three hours
Workshop designed for parents, guardians and teachers which
examines the level of customer service given to children

- Identifies and addresses the attitudes and behaviors adults bring that could make children want to "do business elsewhere"
- Focuses on discipline, communication, time management and family activities
- Utilizes a self assessment/evaluation that allows adults to examine the level of service given to a child

"Customer Service in God's House"
Leadership Edition

Sessions vary from a three-hour workshop to a two-day retreat
A comprehensive real-life reality check for new and existing leaders
which explores a continuous leadership improvement plan that
addresses the skills, gifting and willingness a leader must bring to
the table in order to be an effective influence

- Leadership Self-Assessment
- Time and Energy Management
- Effective Communication Skills
- Using What You Already Have
- I Built It But No One Came
- Equipping and Empowering Your Team
- Uncovering the Terrorists Within
- From Terrorist to Team Player

Methodology

These workshop sessions incorporate the following: Group
discussions, brief lectures, videos, *real life* role-plays, games, self-
assessment and evaluations, field trips and a variety of planned and
impromptu activities that keep participants continuously stimulated
and motivated during training sessions. Follow up training is
available for those clients who may require a small group setting or
one-on-one refresher training, mentoring or coaching.

About the Author

Roz Tandy is the owner and training director of the Luke Agency, a customer service, job readiness, entrepreneurial and leadership organization. She began her company in 1998 and is committed to promoting attitudes that will raise the standards and expectations a person has of themselves and others. Her dedication, knowledge and vast experiences have made her a highly regarded trainer, facilitator, motivational speaker and presenter.

She was employed for over thirty-five years in sales, clerical and customer service environments. She has walked in the shoes of many of those persons desiring the skill sets and finesse needed to acquire and maintain long-term employment, business ownership and leadership savvy. Her sensitivity to where they are makes her all the more effective.

Her teaching is designed to meet people where they are and to get them moving in the direction they are destined to be. Roz has continued to develop and expand this gift by remembering that the best place to learn is in the front of the class as the instructor. She believes *'it is never too late to be what you could have become'*.

Roz is the author of two other published works entitled, *"Discovering My Greatness"* and the first edition of *"Customer Service in God's House"* published in 2004.

Breinigsville, PA USA
01 October 2009
225076BV00001B/3/P